To Rosemary
Courtney,

with every good
wish,

George Sullivan
9/9/73

The Complete Book of
Autograph Collecting

GEORGE SULLIVAN

The Complete Book of Autograph Collecting

Illustrated

DODD, MEAD & COMPANY
New York

ACKNOWLEDGMENTS

A good number of autograph dealers and organization officials were helpful in providing background information and autograph reproductions for use in this book. Special thanks are due the following. Conway Barker, La Marque, Texas; Herman Darvick, Brooklyn, New York; Paul V. Lutz, Editor, *Manuscripts*, Tyler, Texas; Kenneth W. Duckett, Executive Secretary, The Manuscript Society, Carbondale, Illinois; Doris Harris, Los Angeles, California; Charles Hamilton, New York City; Dr. Milton Kronovet, Brooklyn, New York; Paul C. Richards, Brookline, Massachusetts; and George Reynolds, New York City.

Many autograph collectors were also especially cooperative, among them: A. J. Cavallaro, Lake Ronkonkoma, New York; Paul Hartunian, Belleville, New Jersey; Dicky Ow, Santa Cruz, California; Max Schrager, Los Angeles, California; Frank Schapitl, Wharton, New Jersey; Peter Shikes, Barrington, New Jersey; Doris Schiff, New York City; Nathaniel E. Stein, New York City; and William J. Sullivan, Springfield, Massachusetts.

ILLUSTRATION CREDITS

Fleet Publishing Co. © 1957, 22 (top and bottom); King Features Syndicate © 1970, 68; The National Archives, 124; The New York Public Library, 5, 7, 9, 55, 81, 97, 103, 105, 121; Parke-Bernet Galleries, 111; Paul Richards, 110; George Sullivan, 2, 6, 13, 14, 18, 21, 90, 130, 131, 134; Wagner International Photos, Inc., 16.

Contents

I was at a luncheon honoring President
Kennedy when word was received that
there had been an accident and the Governor
and the President had been taken to the
hospital. The luncheon broke up and on
the way out I heard that he had been
shot and had died.

I went home and phoned my office.
The U. S. attorney was there and he came
on the line and said the vice-president
was on the other line and wanted me
to give him the oath of office. I got
in my car, hurried to the airport and
with Mrs. Kennedy on his left and
Mrs. Johnson on his right he repeated
the oath. I immediately left the plane.

Sarah T. Hughes

In this response to a letter from a collector, Federal Judge Sarah T. Hughes, who administered the oath of office to Lyndon B. Johnson after President Kennedy's assassination, reviews the events of November 22, 1963. (FROM THE COLLECTION OF HERMAN DARVICK)

1 *"A Delectable Hobby"*

L ATE IN 1968, a twenty-two-year-old Brooklyn, New York, school teacher and autograph collector named Herman Darvick wrote a short letter to Federal Judge Sarah T. Hughes that contained a probing question. It was Judge Hughes who administered the oath of office to Lyndon B. Johnson on the afternoon of November 22, 1963, aboard the presidential airliner, *Air Force One*, while it stood on the runway at Love Field near Dallas.

"Would you be good enough to write and tell me your impressions of that day?" asked Mr. Darvick.

A few weeks later he received a reply in the form of a single-page, handwritten letter on Judge Hughes' official stationery. "I was at a luncheon meeting honoring President Kennedy when word was received that there had been an accident and the Governor and the President had been taken to the hospital," the letter began. It then went on to tell, clearly and exactly, the events experienced by Judge Hughes that day.

Mr. Darvick treasures Judge Hughes' letter—and no wonder. It is a behind-the-scenes look at a momentous day in American history. More than that, it is an actual, physical link with those fateful hours.

This is what autograph collecting is all about.

Autograph collecting is, as dealer Charles Hamilton calls it,

A "private moment" with quarterback Joe Namath.

one of the most "personal" of all hobbies. "It's one," he says, "that brings a person close to the great men and women of the past, not only to their handwriting and the very page on which they set down their emotions and ideas, but their most intimate thoughts. . . . It is," says Mr. Hamilton, "a delectable hobby."

To most people the word "autograph" means simply a person's signature. (The word is derived from the Greek *autos*, meaning self, and *graphein*, to write.) But to collectors and autograph dealers, the word has a much wider meaning. Besides mere signatures, autograph material can refer to almost anything that is handwritten or typed, whether or not it bears a signature. Any note or letter is regarded as autograph material.

It can be any signed document, such as a will, a deed, a check, a military discharge, or a land grant. Autograph material can be a book manuscript, notes of music set down by a composer, or a sketch by an artist. Lincoln's Gettysburg Address is autograph material, as is a signed copy of the Declaration of Independence or even a printed copy of the Declaration of Independence, although the last named is considered so only by virtue of its association with the signers of the Declaration, and thus would be known as "association material."

In its most elementary form, the hobby involves collecting the signatures of the world's celebrities. Those who pursue collecting on this level are often to be seen outside the stage doors of television studios, legitimate theaters, and lecture halls, and they are extremely active at baseball parks, proferring their small albums or scraps of paper to the people they feel to be important.

An American novelist describes this as "a primitive form of behavior, being excusable only because the principals are still at a primitive stage." A prominent author calls it a "nutty form of acquisitiveness."

Even though this category of collecting is not held in high esteem by advanced collectors, millions of people indulge in it, from street urchins to kings and dictators. At a banquet given by Winston Churchill at the time of the Potsdam Conference during World War II, the last meeting of the three Allied chiefs of state, Churchill's menu was passed around for signatures. At the very same time, Russian premier Joseph V. Stalin was circling the table getting his own collection of signatures.

Why do people collect signatures? One young man explains it this way: "When someone signs an autograph for you, it's as if you have a private moment with that person. It may be only a few seconds, but you never forget it. You know that person, really know him, because of it."

The signed slip of paper becomes the physical evidence of

that "private moment." It is certain to be displayed and shown to one's friends.

Another great segment of collectors obtain autograph material by mail, writing the world's notables in every field—government and science, art and music. They may request a signed photograph or, better, an inscription in a book, or a comment in a letter on our life and times. On this level, autograph collecting is much more highly regarded.

Then there are the so-called "serious" collectors, those who build their collections by buying material from one or more of the country's approximately forty active autograph dealers. These collectors limit their efforts to one field, or several of them, in which they become expert. A collector of Civil War autograph material is likely to know as much about the historical background of the conflict, its battles, the peace, and the years of reconstruction as a college professor.

Another category of collectors are investors. "I buy at least one good piece of presidential material every month," says one. "The prices keep going up. It's a much better investment than the stock market."

There is no sharp division between categories, and almost all collectors are active in at least two of them. The autograph "hound," besides besieging celebrities on the street, may also write letters requesting signatures or photographs, and the more advanced collector, although he may acquire most of his material by purchase, is also likely to correspond with notables, with people included in his specialty.

The very first thing you should do as a beginner is develop a plan, a long-term goal. Maybe it will be very modest in scope, like collecting the signatures of all the living members of baseball's Hall of Fame. Or it can be something quite splendid, such as gathering the signatures of all the United States presidents, or the signers of the Declaration of Independence.

You may want to become a "subject collector," building a

collection of material devoted to a central theme, such as the Civil War or the American West. If this is the case, you'll be concerned primarily with content of documents, and less so with the name of the signer.

What type of collecting you do doesn't matter. What is important is that you follow a blueprint. You should specialize, devoting your attention to a particular subject or subjects. There is a long list of topics from which you can choose. Some of them are listed below:

Architecture	Government	Motion pictures
Art	History	Music
Astronautics	Industry	Politics
Aviation	International relations	Publishing
Business	Journalism	Radio
Dance	Labor	Religion
Diplomacy	Law	Social science
Education	Literature	Sports
Engineering	Medicine	Television
Finance	Military	Theater

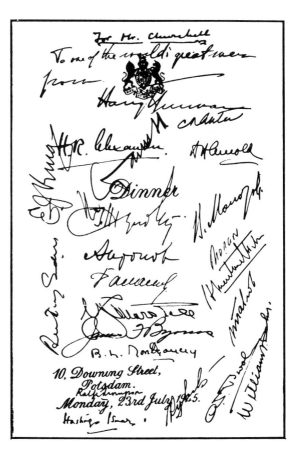

A reproduction of Churchill's autograph menu, with signatures gathered at a dinner given during the Potsdam Conference.

Some of these subjects are too broad to consider in themselves. You must further specialize. For example, American history offers such specialties as Revolutionary War generals, Civil War generals, military leaders of World War I or II, the Old West, Indians, the Gold Rush, slavery, military discharges, pioneers, and railroads. The list is endless.

A young woman might specialize in autograph material representing the First Ladies or wives of the presidents. Distinguished women writers, artists, or scientists are other categories to consider.

Award winners and prize winners make interesting categories. The Nobel Prize, perhaps the most esteemed award in the world, is given annually to those who "have conferred the greatest benefit on mankind" in each of six fields: chemistry, economics, literature, peace, physics, and medicine-physiology. The Nobel Prizes were first awarded in 1901, so there are scores of recipients whose autograph material you can collect. The Pulitzer

Prizes are highly regarded, too. These are awarded in the fields of journalism, letters, and music, and were first given in 1917.

Many thousands of other awards are conferred each year by various civic, professional, academic, and government organizations. The National Institute of Arts and Letters honors distinguished artists, composers, and writers; the National Book Awards are presented annually to the authors of the most distinguished books; and each year the president presents the National Medal of Science to individuals for outstanding contributions in the physical, biological, mathematical, and engineering sciences. The motion picture industry has the Academy Awards; the theater, the Antoinette Perry (Tony)

Notes of music signed by the composer are one type of autograph material.

Awards; music, the Grammy Awards; and television, the Emmy Awards.

Recipients of these awards and prizes are listed in the many different yearbooks and almanacs available at your library. Each group of award winners can serve as a collecting category, or serve as a guide to the names of the leading figures in any given field.

Keep alert to current events and you'll find new subjects constantly suggesting themselves. The Negroes' struggle to gain full legal, economic, and social equality has opened countless fields. New personalities are continually coming to the forefront; Neil Armstrong and Spiro Agnew were virtual "unknowns" until relatively recent times.

No matter what specialty you choose, it should reflect your interests and tastes, and even your personality. If you enjoy reading Ogden Nash, but find Wallace Stevens a puzzle, then collect Nash items. If you are studying Spanish in school and the history of Latin America interests you, then consider collecting items signed by the presidents and dictators of South America.

When making a decision as to your specialty, it's a good idea to consult an autograph dealer or an experienced collector. If there is no dealer in your area, write to one and ask his opinion. (Dealer addresses are listed in the appendix.) Dealers are good about answering queries. The Universal Autograph Collectors Club or The Manuscript Society (see below) will furnish you with the names of collectors in your area.

Visit your local library and read the books available on the subject of collecting. Perhaps the best is *Autographs: A Key to Collecting* by Mary A. Benjamin, a leading dealer. It is a carefully written and comprehensive view of the field. *Word Shadows of the Great* by Thomas Madigan is another all-embracing study by an author who knew the autograph field thoroughly. A third recommended title is *Collecting Autographs and Manu-*

Editor Scribner's Monthly

Dear Sir

I have read the paper by Mr Francis Upton and it is the first correct and authoritative account of my invention of the Electric Light

Yours Truly

Thomas A Edison.

Menlo Park N.J.

Any letter, handwritten or typed, is autograph material.

scripts by Charles Hamilton. It gives valuable insights into several aspects of collecting. The names of other books on collecting are listed in the appendix.

Once you start collecting, there are two organizations you should consider joining. One is the Universal Autograph Collectors Club, an organization founded in 1965 to "advance the interests of autograph collectors and popularize the art and study of autograph collecting."

To join the UACC, write to Herman Darvick (3109 Brighton 7th Street, Brooklyn, New York 11235) and request an application form. Dues are $6.00 a year. Anyone interested in autographs is eligible for membership.

When you become a member, you receive a subscription to *The Pen and Quill*, the organization's monthly newspaper. Each issue contains articles by members concerning their collections and collecting experiences, tips on preserving and mounting autographs, and the addresses for a dozen or so of the world's notables.

The other collectors' organization is The Manuscript Society. One of its chief goals is to "encourage the meeting of autograph collectors and stimulate and aid them in their various collecting specialties." The organization also seeks to "facilitate the exchange of information and knowledge among researchers, schools, and collectors," and to "foster the greater use of original manuscript source material in the study, teaching, and writing of history." Its membership includes collectors, dealers, librarians, historical societies, colleges, and other individuals interested in collecting. It has about one thousand members.

Annual membership is $10.00 a year for adults. A special student membership is available at $4.00. For a membership application, write to: Kenneth Duckett, Executive Secretary, The Manuscript Society (Morris Library, Southern Illinois University, Carbondale, Illinois 62901).

Members receive without charge the organization's quarterly publication, *Manuscripts.* Each issue contains news about collecting, information on newly discovered material, book reviews, and a special feature entitled "The Young Collector," usually written by a high school or college student. Collectors seeking specialized manuscript material are invited to place advertisements noting their "wants" in the publication.

Besides publishing *Manuscripts,* the Society sponsors exhibits of autograph material throughout the country, conducts chapter meetings in various cities, and once each year holds a three-day convention for members. The site is a section of the country of particular interest to collectors because of local manuscript resources.

The Pen and Quill and *Manuscripts* are the publications that will help you the most, but there are some others you may wish to read. Each issue of *Hobbies: The Magazine for Collectors* (1006 South Michigan Avenue, Chicago, Illinois 60605) features at least one article on the subject of autographs. A one-year subscription costs $5.00, and a sample issue 50¢.

Dealer Mary A. Benjamin (790 Madison Avenue, New York, New York 10021) publishes a magazine with news and background information on autograph collecting. Titled *The Collector*, it also describes autograph material for sale. Subscription rates: six issues, $5.00.

The below listed publications contain classified advertisements about buying and swapping autographs:

Collectors' Den (Box 5525, San Antonio, Texas 78201), one year, 12 issues, $3.00.
Collectors News (Box 156, Grundy Center, Iowa 50638), one year, 12 issues, $3.00.
Collector's Weekly (Kermit, Texas 79745), one year, 52 issues, $4.00; sample copy, 35¢.
The Flea Marketeer (800 W. 7 Mile Road, Detroit, Michigan 48023), one year, 12 issues, $2.50; sample copy, 35¢.

Autograph collecting is not like collecting glass marbles or political campaign buttons. Each signature, letter, or document that you acquire should have a special meaning, and each should serve to both educate and enrich you.

"You should look upon autograph collecting in the same way an engineer looks upon the construction of a bridge," says one dealer. "Without a plan, the steel for the bridge would pile up in meaningless stacks. But the engineer fits the pieces of steel together in such a way that he creates a structure, one not only of practical value, but often one of great beauty."

So it should be with autograph collecting. Each acquisition should be like finding a piece to a puzzle. Each should be an enriching experience. Then collecting will truly be a "delectable hobby."

2 Getting Autographs in Person

MANY YOUNGSTERS have an avid interest in sports, and often the very first autographs they ever acquire are those of baseball or football stars. Most athletes are cooperative about granting autographs. This, plus the fact that virtually every section of the country is now represented by a professional team of some kind, makes sports a recommended category for the beginning collector.

In seeking sports autographs, it's wise to limit yourself to the major *professional* sports—baseball, football, basketball, and ice hockey. The field of amateur sports seldom produces personalities whose signatures are worthwhile from a collector's standpoint.

Never be hesitant about asking a professional athlete for his signature. League and team officials encourage players to cooperate with fans. "No matter how tired you are, sign autographs," a commissioner of the American Football League used to tell teams. "Remember the days when you were a kid looking up to an athlete and how much an autograph meant to you." In baseball, many clubs schedule Autograph Days on which players are stationed somewhere in the park before game time for the purpose of signing.

Many baseball players sign autographs before the game begins. This is Bobby Murcer of the Yankees.

It has been estimated that about three players out of every four are cooperative about signing. "Of course, I sign," says Johnny Unitas, quarterback of the Baltimore Colts. "I know how much an autograph means to a youngster. I couldn't refuse."

In his book, *Ball Four*, former New York Yankee pitcher Jim Bouton says, "I get a tremendous kick out of people wanting my autograph. In fact, I feel hurt if I go some place where I think I should be recognized and no one asks for me." Countless other players feel the same.

Players often sign autographs at the park before the game begins. Some teams permit the players to sign right up until game time, while other teams have different deadlines. The American League has a rule which prohibits players from signing "while the game is in progress."

Pitcher Mel Stottlemyre signs after a game at Yankee Stadium.

When requesting an autograph, remember that courtesy counts. Address the players as you would any adult. Frank Robinson is *Mister* Robinson, not Frank. Pete Rose is *Mister* Rose, not Pete or Rose.

"Players don't like being called by their last names," says Carl Morton, a pitcher for the Montreal Expos. "More players would be willing to sign if the kids called them 'Mister.'"

It is also possible to obtain autographs outside the stadium before or after a game, as players are arriving or departing. After a game is a better time than before, and requesting autographs from players of a winning team is usually more fruitful than pursuing losers.

Your favorite team's training facility is an excellent place to obtain autographs. In the case of a baseball team, this refers to the base—usually in Florida or Arizona—where the players

14

work out each spring in preparation for the season ahead. Professional football and basketball teams begin training in late summer and usually utilize college facilities. Virtually all training camps are open to the public. When not actually involved in training sessions, players have time to talk to fans, pose for pictures, and sign autographs.

Players also sign autographs when making promotion appearances, such as at the opening of a sporting goods store, a supermarket, or in connection with a product the athlete may endorse. Indeed, signing autographs is often the primary activity of the player when making such appearances.

Veteran autograph collectors get most of their signatures at the hotel where the visiting team stays when on the road. For example, when the Pittsburgh Pirates travel to New York City to play the Mets, the team stays at the Hotel Commodore. Collectors never fail to congregate there.

It's the same with other teams in other cities. To find out where teams stay when on the road, consult *The Official Baseball Guide*, published by *The Sporting News* (1212 N. Lindbergh Boulevard, St. Louis, Missouri 63166). Published annually in April, it costs $2.00.

The best time to approach the players is just before the team bus leaves the hotel for the stadium. The bus usually pulls up in front of the hotel about three hours before the scheduled time of the game. You should arrange to be at the hotel about half an hour before the bus arrives. Approach the players as they come through the lobby or on the sidewalk in front of the hotel.

Teams in all major sports operate in this fashion. Remember, however, the athletes are wearing street clothes, not their uniforms, and unless you are a dedicated fan, they may be difficult to identify.

"Baseball players are the easiest to recognize because you know their faces from television, bubble gum cards, and the pictures that appear in sports magazines," says one collector.

"Pro basketball players are no problem either because they're exceptionally tall and they carry their own duffel bags.

"But you have problems trying to recognize pro football players. Each squad is large, consisting of forty men or so, and usually only the quarterback, a couple of running backs, and one or two receivers are well known. The rest look like ordinary businessmen.

"Hockey players are a problem, too. Only a few of the game's superstars are recognizable."

Whenever you approach a player, ask him to sign something more interesting than a scrap of paper, a scorecard or program, or an index card. Signatures in a conventional autograph book are not much better.

It's far more exciting to have the player sign a picture. Many youngsters cut out the color portraits that appear in *Sport* magazine each month and present them to the appropriate sports stars for autographing. Color pictures are also printed in *Sports Illustrated* and in the various yearbooks that cover the sports scene. Check your local newsstand for these.

Players almost never fail to sign autographs when making promotion appearances. This is Earl Morrall of the Baltimore Colts.

1969 Monaco Hardtop

Earl Morrall will pass the word about Dodge Fever.

Earl Morrall

Earl Morrall—NFL's Most Valuable Player ('68-'69).

This is the card Earl Morrall signed.

There is another source of pictures you should know about. Besides their affiliation with a professional team, many pro athletes are also under contract to a company that manufactures sports equipment. For example, Johnny Bench of the Cincinnati Reds also represents the Rawlings Sporting Goods company. Tennis star Dennis Ralston represents the Spalding company.

Write to one or more of the various companies that manufacture sporting goods equipment, and ask them to send photographs of their advisory staff members. They'll be happy to do so. Here is a listing of the leading manufacturers and their addresses:

Rawlings Sporting Goods
2300 Delmar Boulevard
St. Louis, Missouri 63166

Wilson Sporting Goods
2233 West Street
River Grove, Illinois 60171

Spalding Bros. Inc.
Meadow Street
Chicopee, Massachusetts 01013

MacGregor-Brunswick Inc.
623 S. Wabash Avenue
Chicago, Illinois 60605

Should you ask a player to inscribe or dedicate a photograph to you personally? It depends. There isn't the slightest doubt that a photograph that says, "To John Smith, with best wishes,

Collectors surround Pittsburgh pitcher Steve Blass outside New York's Hotel Commodore.

Bob Gibson," is much more revered by John Smith than a photograph that is signed simply "Bob Gibson." However, the dollar value of the inscribed photograph will be slightly less than the one that is not inscribed. The reason is that one individual doesn't particularly want an item that's dedicated to someone else. So if you are thinking only of showing and displaying the photograph, ask to have it inscribed. But if your interest is in selling or trading the item, a signature alone is best.

Many youngsters collect signatures on baseballs. If you plan to do this, carry the ball in a plastic bag to and from the stadium or in the box in which it was originally packaged. This will prevent the signatures from becoming smudged.

Other youngsters collect autographs in baseball or football record manuals, having each athlete sign just above or below his statistical entry. Use your imagination and you'll think of other items that make for meaningful souvenirs. In 1970, when Sam McDowell of the Cleveland Indians won his twentieth game, one enterprising young man had a Xerox copy made of

18

the newspaper story about the event and then got McDowell to sign it.

Naturally, it's up to you to furnish the pen the celebrity uses in signing. A ball-point pen is merely adequate. While the ink supply is long-lasting, a ball-point pen will sometimes skip and leave gaps, especially when a photograph or other slick-surfaced piece of material is being signed. It is much better to use a pen with a fiber or bonded nylon tip. The pen with the bonded nylon tip never fails to give a bold signature, one that is much more striking in appearance than the ball-point pen type. One pen of this kind is sold under the trade name "Flair!," and sells in five-and-ten-cent stores for about fifty cents.

Not every player signs, of course. Some simply don't have the time for collectors. Others are fearful of being mobbed.

One way to cope with the athlete in a hurry is to carry a supply of postal cards in your pocket, each one addressed to yourself. Simply hand one to the player, saying, "Please sign this when you have time, and then mail it to me." This strategy

Sporting goods companies send out free photographs like this one.

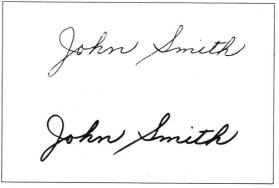

Fiber-tipped pens give a bolder, more desirable signature, as shown in the lower signature here.

works with surprising success, and it can be applied to celebrities of any type, not just professional sports stars.

Another ingenious method was used with success by a trio of Jackson Heights, New York, girls. They took a large sheet of heavy white cardboard, and in one corner lettered in big type the message, "Hi! Please sign!" Before home games of the New York Mets at Shea Stadium, they hung their sign on the low fence that separates players and fans. Scores of players complied with their lettered plea.

Another ploy is to tie a length of cord to one's autograph book and then, before—not during—a game, hang the book over the dugout roof so that the players within can see it. Use a short length of cord to attach a pen to the book cover. This scheme produces only mixed results, however.

A Long Island, New York, collector employs this strategy to obtain signatures of the New York Yankees: He writes a letter requesting an autograph to a particular member of the team, then places it in an envelope, which he addresses to the player. He also encloses a self-addressed stamped envelope.

He then takes the envelope and tosses it onto the field at Yankee Stadium before a game. More often than not, somebody picks it up—sometimes it is another player; other times a member of the ground crew—reads the address, then turns it over to the addressee, the player. "The autograph arrives in the mail in two or three days," the collector says.

Much of what has been said about sports figures applies to celebrities in other fields. If you read in the newspaper that a Hollywood star or noted television personality is going to visit your city, learn all you can about the star's schedule. What time is he going to arrive? At what hotel will he be staying? Where and when are his appearances scheduled?

The first opportunity for a signature is at the airline terminal. Usually the celebrity will sign autographs before taking his limousine into the city.

Collectors never fail to concentrate their efforts upon the hotel where the celebrity stays. When the Beatles visited New York City at the height of their fame, police barriers had to be erected outside the Hotel Warwick to keep their fans under control.

Broadway stars usually sign autographs outside the stage door of the theater where they are appearing. This is Zsa Zsa Gabor.

Columnist Earl Wilson's signature strikes a whimsical note.

"It's usual for one of us to call the star's hotel room on a house telephone," says one collector, "and ask what time he or she will be coming through the lobby. You usually get a secretary or an assistant who is happy to give you the information."

In the case of stars of the legitimate stage, collectors wait outside the theater. The star signs at the stage door on his way into the theater, about an hour before curtain time, and after the performance as well.

Naturally, any time you visit movie or television production facilities you are likely to be presented with countless opportunities for autographs. A young man who toured Universal Studios in Hollywood described it as a "collector's paradise." He marveled at the fact that stars seemed to "walk around all day signing autographs."

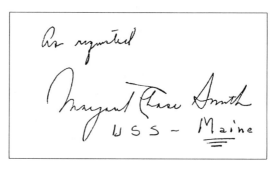

Margaret Chase Smith, United States senator from Maine, emphasizes her state in her autograph.

3 *Writing for Signatures*

AN EXTRAORDINARY number of the world's notables are prepared to send their signatures by mail. They are yours for the asking. All you have to do is make a request.

To begin, buy envelopes and matching writing paper at the five-and-ten or a stationery store. You can use post cards, obtainable at the post office, in sending out your requests, but letters produce better results and the cost is only a tiny bit more.

There's no need to typewrite the letters. Handwritten letters are fine, as long as your penmanship can be easily read.

What should your letter say? One veteran collector gives this advice:

- Be polite.
- Be concise.
- A little flattery helps, but don't overdo it.

Some collectors prepare their letter and have copies printed, or duplicated by mimeograph. They then fill in the name of the addressee, sign the letter, and send it out. This has to be considered bad manners. There's no excuse for not sending a personal note, either handwritten or typewritten.

Be sure to enclose a stamped, self-addressed envelope. This advice must be heeded. Most people in private life do not have the funds to pay the postage fees involved in fulfilling autograph

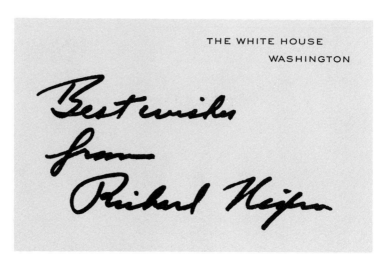

President Richard M. Nixon answers collectors' requests with a card like this one.

requests. The expense can run to thousands of dollars a year.

There's an exception to this rule, however. There's no need to enclose postage when writing to people in political life. The president, the vice-president, members of the cabinet, members of both Houses of Congress, and other high government officials have been granted the franking privilege, which means that their printed signature in the upper right-hand corner of an envelope ensures that their letters will be transmitted free. State and municipal officials have funds for this purpose.

You don't have to limit your requests to people in the United States. Well-known figures in foreign countries will send you their signatures, too.

Writing to foreign countries can be expensive, however. You will want to use air mail—surface mail is so slow it takes the excitement out of writing—and the letter itself, plus the postage you enclose, can bring the cost to about seventy-five cents a letter.

When writing to someone in a foreign country use International Reply Coupons instead of enclosing United States postage stamps. All United States post offices sell International Reply

24

Mrs. Nixon's signature on autograph cards is likely to be genuine, say experts.

Coupons. They cost fifteen cents each. If you judge that the return postage on a letter is going to be thirty cents, enclose two International Reply Coupons. The person receiving the coupons redeems them at his local post office for stamps.

Whenever you receive a reply, open the envelope carefully, slitting it across the top with a letter opener. Keep the envelope. Also save any correspondence that accompanies a signed photograph, or any note, typed as well as handwritten, that might be included with a signature card. Store any material of this type just as carefully as you do the autograph itself. It may be important one day in establishing the authenticity of the signature.

Whom you write to depends on your field of interest, your specialty. Many new collectors begin by writing to high government officials—the president, the vice-president, members of the president's cabinet, supreme court justices, senators, or members of the House of Representatives.

The names and addresses of top-level government officials are easy to obtain. In the case of the cabinet, write and request a listing from the Cabinet Secretary (The White House Office,

Requests to Vice-President Spiro T. Agnew bring this photograph.

Washington, D. C. 20500). For the members of the Senate, write to The Chief Clerk (The Senate, Washington, D. C. 20510), and for the House of Representatives, write to Clerk (The House of Representatives, Washington, D. C. 20515).

Names and addresses of all government officials are also to be found in any one of the various almanacs or yearbooks available in libraries and bookstores. These include *The World Almanac, The Information Please Almanac,* and *The Reader's Digest Almanac and Yearbook.* Each costs about $2.00.

An even better source, certainly a more comprehensive one, is the *United States Government Organization Manual.* An 820-page paperback book that undergoes revision annually, the manual is offered for sale by the Superintendent of Documents (Government Printing Office, Washington, D. C. 20402) at $3.00 a copy.

When writing, always use the proper form of address, as follows:

THE PRESIDENT
Envelope address:
    The President
    The White House
    Washington, D. C.
Salutation:
    Mr. President,

THE VICE-PRESIDENT
Envelope address:
    Vice-President (full name)
    Executive Office Building
    Washington, D. C. 20502
Salutation:
    Dear Sir,

CABINET OFFICERS
Envelope address:
    The Honorable (full name of cabinet officer)
    The Secretary of (name of department)
    The Department of _____
    Washington, D. C. (zip code)
Salutation:
    Dear Mr. (or Madame) Secretary,

CHIEF JUSTICE OF THE SUPREME COURT
Envelope address:
    The Chief Justice of the United States (full name)
    The Supreme Court of the United States
    Washington, D. C. 20543
Salutation:
    Dear Mr. Chief Justice,

JUSTICES OF THE SUPREME COURT
Envelope address:
    Mr. Justice (last name)
    The Supreme Court of the United States
    Washington, D. C. 20543
Salutation:
    Dear Mr. Justice,

27

SENATORS
Envelope address:
  The Honorable (full name)
  United States Senate
  Washington, D. C. 20510
Salutation:
  Dear Senator (last name),

REPRESENTATIVES
Envelope address:
  The Honorable (name)
  House of Representatives
  Washington, D. C. 20515
Salutation:
  Dear Mr. (last name),

GOVERNORS
Envelope address:
  The Honorable (name)
  Governor of (name of state)
  State Capitol Building
  (city, state, zip code)
Salutation:
  Dear Governor (last name),

If you write to the president requesting an autograph, it is likely you will receive in return a small card, slightly larger than a business card, imprinted with the words "The White House," and bearing the president's signature under the salutation, "Best wishes." Sending out such cards was the policy in the Kennedy, Johnson, and Nixon administrations.

The signature that appears on the card is not genuine in the sense that the president has actually signed it. It is likely to be a printed signature, or it may be one mechanically produced by a device called an Autopen.

If you write to the president's wife, you are more likely to receive a genuine signature. "Mrs. Nixon places primary importance on her correspondence, with particular emphasis to mail received from young people," Constance Stuart, Staff

Arkansas' Senator J. W. Fulbright sends admirers this signed portrait.

J w Fulbright
1970

Below: "Aloha from Hawaii!" says Congresswoman Patsy T. Mink.

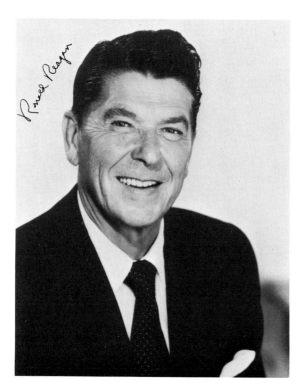

Many collectors specialize in governors. This is California's Ronald Reagan.

Director to Mrs. Nixon, once said. "We have never known her to fail to comply with a request for an autograph."

Since it is virtually impossible to obtain an original signature of the president by means of a letter of request, many collectors attempt to obtain autograph material from the "next president." Who will be the presidential candidates of the future? That's the question to ask yourself. Early in 1971, Senator Birch Bayh of Indiana, Senator George McGovern of South Dakota, Senator Edmund Muskie of Maine, Senator Edward "Ted" Kennedy of Massachusetts, and Mayor John Lindsay of New York were among the leading contenders. The idea, of course, is to obtain a letter or signed photograph from each of the presidential hopefuls. No matter which one emerges the eventual winner, you will have an authentic presidential signature.

The chief contenders begin to become visible about a year

before the actual election takes place. For instance, in September, 1967, it was believed that the party nominees for president and vice-president in the fall of 1968 would come from a group that included Hubert Humphrey and Robert Kennedy among the Democrats, and George Romney, Richard Nixon, Ronald Reagan, Charles Percy, and Nelson Rockefeller among the Republicans. At that time—the fall of 1967—it was possible to obtain autographed photographs of each one of these men (although some of these photographs might have been signed by the Autopen.) Those collectors who had the foresight to send out requests to Richard Nixon now have a valuable signature.

Every collector interested in presidential signatures always makes it a point to collect autograph material from the vice-president. The reason, of course, is that the vice-president might become the next president.

During his tenure as vice-president, Lyndon Johnson was most generous in sending out autograph material bearing his original signature. Upon becoming president, he turned to the Autopen.

Members of Congress are wonderfully cooperative in answering autograph requests. Most senators and representatives respond with a signed 8″ x 10″ photograph. Sometimes the photograph is larger; occasionally it is a color photograph.

If you decide to collect letters or photographs from senators, you may obtain several items that increase in value as time passes. Suppose you were collecting senatorial autographs in 1960. You would have obtained the signatures of two future presidents—John Kennedy and Lyndon Johnson—and a future vice-president—Hubert Humphrey.

The governors of the fifty states are also cooperative. Some governors—Ronald Reagan of California, Nelson Rockefeller of New York, and George Wallace of Alabama—have important national stature, and their signed photographs are well worth obtaining.

Japanese characters grace the signed photograph of Ambassador Senjin Tsuruoka, Japan's representative to the United Nations.

The chief justice of the United States and the associate justices often honor requests for autograph material, as do most American military leaders. General William C. Westmoreland, Chief of Staff, United States Army, who played an important role in the Viet Nam conflict, willingly responds. Mail to high-ranking military personnel should be addressed to the individual in care of The Pentagon (Washington, D. C. 20301).

Sometimes royal personages answer autograph requests, although in many cases two or three letters are necessary in order to convince the individual that you are indeed a worthy recipient. Often, too, you must wait a long time for a reply, sometimes longer than three months. Another factor: Since you are writing to a foreign country, postage rates are substantially higher. You encounter similar problems when writing to any of the foreign heads of state, not necessarily royalty. But what you eventually earn in the way of a reply is well worth whatever travail you're caused and the added expense.

Persistence pays. In 1966, Herman Darvick, later president of the Universal Autograph Collectors Club, wrote to President Charles de Gaulle of France and asked for his autograph. Darvick's letter expressed his admiration of the French general and saluted him for his contributions on behalf of France and the French people. A few weeks later Darvick received an answer from de Gaulle's secretary saying that the French leader did not give autographs.

Darvick took the letter as a challenge. "I decided to make a project out of getting de Gaulle's signature," he says.

Ballerina Maria Tallchief answers collectors with this photograph.

JACK MITCHELL
NYC

Next, he sent de Gaulle a first-day cover bearing a stamp which honored the United States Army and pictured American troops parading through the Arc de Triomphe. Darvick had been successful in having both Dwight D. Eisenhower and Omar Bradley, the generals who headed the United States armed forces in Europe during World War II, autograph the cover, and he felt that de Gaulle could not refuse to add his name.

But de Gaulle did refuse. The cover was returned to Darvick with a letter from de Gaulle's secretary reminding him of the general's policy of not giving autographs.

Darvick would not give up. He decided to appeal to de Gaulle's secretary, the man who had been writing him. His name was X. de Beaulaincourt. Darvick went to the Brooklyn Public Library and looked up his home address in the Paris telephone directory. He then sent de Beaulaincourt a registered letter and enclosed half a dozen signatures from his collection, Lyndon Johnson's and Mrs. Johnson's among them. "I'll trade these for a letter or even a signature of General de Gaulle," said Darvick's letter. Again, no success. The signatures were returned with another letter of rebuff.

Darvick made one more attempt. At an auction sale, he purchased a letter signed by Napoleon. He sent this to de Gaulle asking him to sign it, and explained how the students in the fifth grade class he taught had been debating the relative greatness of Napoleon and de Gaulle.

Darvick waited nervously for a reply. Several weeks went by before the mailman delivered a plain white envelope with a French postmark. Darvick slit it open carefully. A three paragraph letter was enclosed. The French leader said he did not wish to sign the Napoleon document, and he then thanked Darvick for his interest.

A letdown? Yes. A disappointment? No. For there at the bottom of the letter was the long sought after signature—"C. de Gaulle."

A letter of request to Prince Rainier III of Monaco often results in a signed post card-size color portrait. It is delivered in an envelope bearing handsome stamps and unusual postmarks. A request to King Faisal of Saudi Arabia is answered by a letter that is delivered by registered mail. It contains the king's signature and a message in Arabic from an aide. Sometimes a letter from a foreign ruler will bear the return address of the country's United Nations mission in New York City, indicating that the letter was sent to the United States by diplomatic courier.

The names and addresses of royal personages and elected government officials of foreign countries are listed in any of the various almanacs mentioned earlier in this chapter. Here is the proper form of address to use when writing:

HEADS OF GOVERNMENT, ROYAL PERSONAGES
Envelope address:
  His (Her) Majesty King (Queen) plus name and appropriate
  Roman numeral
  (capital city)
  (country)
Salutation:
  Your majesty,

HEADS OF GOVERNMENT, ELECTED OFFICIALS
Envelope address:
  His Excellency (full name)
  President of (name of country)
  (capital city)
  (country)
Salutation:
  Your Excellency,

Autograph material from foreign diplomats based in the United States or United Nations ambassadors will add exotic charm to your collection. Diplomatic officials often sign and send out official embassy cards or signed photographs in response to requests.

The names and addresses of all member nations maintaining

permanent missions at United Nations headquarters in New York can be obtained in the book, *Permanent Missions to the United Nations*. You can obtain a copy by writing the United Nations Sales Section, 485 Lexington Avenue, New York, New York 10017. Enclose 75¢, plus 15¢ for handling and mailing.

When writing diplomatic officials, here is the form of address to use:

FOREIGN AMBASSADORS TO THE UNITED STATES
Envelope address:
    His (or Her) Excellency (full name)
    Ambassador of (name of country)
    Embassy of (name of country)
    Washington, D. C. (zip code)
Salutation:
    Dear Mr. (or Mrs.) Ambassador,

AMBASSADORS TO THE UNITED NATIONS
Envelope address:
    His (or Her) Excellency (full name)
    Permanent Representative of (name of country) to the United Nations
    United Nations
    New York, New York 10017
Salutation:
    Dear Mr. (or Mrs.) Ambassador,

Don't fail to consider the lively arts when seeking autographs. Indeed, you may want to concentrate on them. Painting, sculpture, architecture, music, literature, drama, and the dance— each one of these fields offers a bright array of notables for you to write to.

It must be said that it is a bit more difficult to track down the mailing addresses in these fields than it is in the case of United States senators, and the percentage of replies you receive is not likely to be as high as when you write pro football's quarterbacks, but your extra effort and occasional disappointment will be more than offset by the stimulating answers you receive.

Left: *A peace symbol adorns Dustin Hoffman's photograph.* Right: *"Peace," says Dan Rowan of "Laugh-In." However, secretaries usually autograph pictures for their television-star employers.*

Only rarely do people who represent the arts send out photographs. ". . . it seems like just a little too much," says author Norman Mailer. "I never send photos, don't keep them," declares poet Conrad Aiken. "I send autographs *only* if postage is enclosed."

Your local library is sure to have a good-sized shelf of reference books which will provide you with the names and addresses of well-known figures in the arts and sciences. The following books will be most helpful.

Who's Who in America is described as "a biographical dictionary of notable living men and women." In two volumes, the 1970-1971 edition contains more than 2,500 pages and over 68,000 biographical sketches, each one of which includes a mailing address. Those profiled are "key names" in virtually every imaginable field, men and women who have been selected on the basis of occupational position or individual achievement. Here you will find background information on members of Con-

Flip Wilson smiles broadly for admirers.

gress and the president's cabinet, governors of the fifty states, United States ambassadors, heads of major universities and colleges, authors, officers of national and international businesses, and chiefs of state of all nations of the world. Painting, sculpture, classical and folk music, theater, motion pictures, television, and photography are among the fields covered.

No other reference book approaches *Who's Who in America* in the number of people profiled. However, the individual biographical sketches are quite brief, and not likely to be of great help to you in constructing interesting letters of request.

There are also *Who's Who* editions covering France, Germany, and most other European countries, Russia, and even South Africa and Communist China. Incidentally, Michael Collins, Assistant Secretary for Public Affairs of the Department of State, says that "There is no objection on the part of the United States government to the writing of letters by American citizens to leaders in Communist countries, asking for their autographs."

Current Biography Yearbook, published by the H. W. Wilson Company, is an extremely valuable source. It contains, according to the introduction, ". . . objective, accurate, and well-documented articles about living leaders in all fields of human accomplishments." The articles, sometimes several hundred words in length, will provide you with plenty of material useful in helping you to compose interesting letters. *Current Biography Yearbook* also gives the mailing addresses for each person it profiles.

Celebrity Register, published in 1963, contains biographical information on notables in almost every field. A celebrity, states

Baseball's Richie Allen sends out this card; the signature at the bottom is a facsimile, the other is genuine.

angels *Autographs*

Harold "Lefty" Phillips   Ken Tatum   Rudy May

Jim Fregosi   Jarvis Tatum   Tom Murphy

Alex Johnson   Tom Egan   Steve Kealey

Paul Doyle   Ken McMullen   Chico Ruiz

Sandy Alomar   Tom Reynolds   Roger Repoz

Joe Azcue   Ray Oyler   Eddie Fisher

Bill Voss   Mel Queen   Tom Bradley

Jim Spencer   Doug Barnett   Norm Sherry

Jay Johnstone   Dave LaRoche

Clyde Wright   Rocky Bridges
Andy Messersmith

Billy Cowan   Fred Koenig   Pete Reiser

If you write to a baseball or football team and request autographs, you may receive a sheet of facsimile signatures like this one from the California Angels.

the introduction, "is a name which, once made the news, now makes the news itself." The biographical sketches are always interesting and often humorous.

The Blue Book: Leaders of the English Speaking World gives addresses and short biographical sketches for "persons of distinction" from the United States, England, and the British Commonwealth countries. Those listed represent many fields—law, medicine, education, publishing, religion, business, diplomacy, and politics.

Contemporary Authors is a one-volume biographical and bibliographical guide to current authors and their works. Each personal background sketch includes a mailing address.

Twentieth Century Authors, published in 1942, and its First Supplement, published in 1955, offers 2,550 biographical sketches of the authors of all nations.

American Men of Science is an eight-volume biographical directory containing short profiles of men notable for their achievements in research and scholarship in the various scientific fields. Six volumes of the directory are devoted to the physical and biological sciences; two volumes concern the social and behavioral sciences.

Who's Who in American Education is a biographical directory of noted state and national school officers, university and college professors, and superintendents and principals of schools.

There are also directories entitled *Who's Who in American Art*, which covers the fields of painting, sculpturing, illustrating, and cartooning, *Who's Who in Music*, and *Who's Who in the Theater*, and *Who's Who in Finance and Industry*.

If astronautics is your field of interest, you will want to obtain autographed photographs from the members of the United States space team. Almost every collector makes an effort to obtain Neil Armstrong's autographed photograph. As the first man to set foot on the moon. Armstrong will not soon be forgotten. Many collectors also write for the signatures of the "original" astronauts—John Glenn, Jr., Walter M. Schirra, Alan B. Shepard, Leroy G. Cooper, Donald K. Slayton, and M. Scott Carpenter. Virgil I. Grissom, the seventh member of the original space team died in an accidental fire at Cape Kennedy in 1967. Astronaut mail should be addressed to the NASA Manned Spacecraft Center (Houston, Texas 77058). Regrettably, many astronaut signatures are mechanically reproduced by Autopen.

Stars of television and motion pictures, and recording artists, send out autographed photographs in response to requests. Unfortunately, their signatures are almost always signed by secretaries or staff assistants. It's not that the leading show business personalities are any less considerate of their fans than, say, the players who represent the Chicago Cubs. It's simply that these personalities receive such a great number of requests for photographs—literally tons of letters—that it would not be humanly possible to sign each one personally.

This is what fans of Johnny Unitas receive.

JOHN UNITAS

| Baltimore Colts | QB | 6'1'' | 196 | Louisville |

Despite this, you still may want to make an attempt. In the case of the television personalities, address your request in care of the television network on which the star appears. The major networks are:

American Broadcasting Company (ABC-TV)
1330 Avenue of the Americas
New York, New York 10019
    or
4151 Prospect Avenue
Hollywood, California 90027

Columbia Broadcasting System (CBS-TV)
51 West 52nd Street
New York, New York 10019
    or
7800 Beverly Boulevard
Hollywood, California 90036

National Broadcasting Company (NBC-TV)
30 Rockefeller Plaza
New York, New York 10019
    or
3000 West Alameda Avenue
Burbank, California 91503

Flip magazine has compiled a pair of paperback books valuable to anyone seeking autograph material from contemporary musical recording stars. *Flip's Groovy Guide to the Guys* gives biographical information and mailing addresses for one hundred male performers regarded as "the most exciting and entertaining on the teen scene." *Flip's Groovy Guide to the Groops* [*sic*] offers vital statistics, biographical information, and addresses for one hunderd of the leading pop singing groups. These books can be purchased from The New American Library (Box 2310, Grand Central Station, New York, New York 10017). Enclose 75¢ for each book, plus 10¢ to cover mailing.

There are probably more collectors engaged in writing to sports celebrities than those of any other category. In the case of baseball, football, basketball, or ice hockey, letters will reach a player if you simply address the envelope in care of his team and the stadium or area where the team plays. Thus, Hank Aaron's address is:

Mr. Henry "Hank" Aaron
Atlanta Braves
Atlanta Stadium
Atlanta, Georgia 30312

If you wish to write to a retired player but don't know his address, simply address your card or letter in care of the team, or even the league, for which he played. It will be forwarded to him.

The Sporting News (1212 N. Lindbergh Boulevard, St. Louis, Missouri 63166) publishes yearbooks devoted to the various major sports. Each lists players' names and gives complete team addresses. These books include:

The Official Baseball Guide (published in April; $2.00)
The National Football Guide (published in July; $2.00)
Official National Basketball Association Guide (published in October; $1.50)
Official American Basketball Association Guide (published in November; $1.50)
Professional and Senior Hockey Guide (published in October; $2.00)

Teams follow different policies in handling requests for autographs. Some simply do not send out individual players' photographs. They reply to requests with a team picture or an 8″ x 10″ sheet of facsimile signatures of team members.

When you direct your autograph request to an individual player, it will be complied with more often than not. Usually club personnel help the player in answering his requests.

"All autograph requests that come to the ball club are answered within a week of the time that they are received," says Jim Schaff, Assistant General Manager of the Kansas City

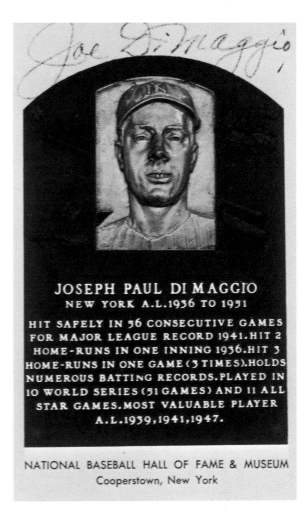

Joe DiMaggio's Hall of Fame "plaque card," autographed by him.

JOSEPH PAUL DI MAGGIO
NEW YORK A.L. 1936 TO 1951

HIT SAFELY IN 56 CONSECUTIVE GAMES FOR MAJOR LEAGUE RECORD 1941. HIT 2 HOME-RUNS IN ONE INNING 1936. HIT 3 HOME-RUNS IN ONE GAME (3 TIMES). HOLDS NUMEROUS BATTING RECORDS. PLAYED IN 10 WORLD SERIES (51 GAMES) AND 11 ALL STAR GAMES. MOST VALUABLE PLAYER A.L. 1939, 1941, 1947.

NATIONAL BASEBALL HALL OF FAME & MUSEUM
Cooperstown, New York

Chiefs. "We provide the players with envelopes and autographed pictures to send out and permit them to use our postage machine in doing it, but the actual stuffing and addressing of the envelopes are their responsibility."

Many other teams in both football and baseball cooperate with their players in much the same fashion. Most provide post card-size photographs for players to sign.

Occasionally sports celebrities send unusual items to people who request their autographs. One collector received three 1965 World Series tickets from a White Sox player. Even though

Chicago didn't play in the World Series that year, the tickets were a much-appreciated souvenir. Another collector received a signed bubble gum card from a player. Dickey Ow, a well-known California collector, received an index card from one-time Red Sox star Eddie Morgan on which Morgan had penciled several batting and fielding tips.

Some players ignore the letters they receive. Willie Mays, the all-star outfielder for the San Francisco Giants, seldom answers autograph requests. However, Stephen Murray, a Rosemont, Pennsylvania, collector, succeeded in getting Mays' signature. Stephen prepared a twenty-page presentation containing photographs of Mays taken from magazines and newspaper clippings, and sent it to the San Francisco slugger. Mays was most grateful. Two weeks later, Stephen received a letter from Mays that said, "Thank you very much for the wonderful report that you prepared about me. I will treasure it with my other precious possessions." And the letter was signed "Willie Mays."

Collector Les Epstein of West Hempstead, New York, was stymied in his efforts to obtain Mickey Mantle's signature until he tried this scheme: He wrote to pitcher Jim Bouton, then a teammate of Mantle, and known by collectors for his many kindnesses, and he explained to Bouton the difficulty he had been having. "Would you please have Mickey sign this card for me?" Epstein's letter said. A few weeks later Bouton returned the card and Mantle's signature was on it.

"Find out who the team 'nice guys' are," says Epstein. "They'll help you." Epstein cites Cincinnati's Pete Rose as one of baseball's most notable "nice guys."

Don't fail to consider the members of the various sports halls of fame when sending out requests for autograph material. The men who have been selected for membership in these national shrines are the most famous of all sports personalities.

While some hall of fame members are deceased, many of the

Vertical stroke signatures, on the left, are those of artists, writers, and composers. Signatures with a right-hand slant, on the right, are those of more extroverted persons.

most glittering "names" are still living, and a majority of them are happy to fulfill autograph requests. Baseball's Hall of Fame and Museum lists as members such "immortals" as Joe DiMaggio, Casey Stengel, and Jackie Robinson. Red Grange, Bronko Nagurski, and Don Hutson are among the members of Pro Football's Hall of Fame.

47

Address autograph requests to the player in care of the appropriate hall of fame. The letter will be forwarded. Here is a list of the principal halls of fame and their addresses:

National Baseball Hall of
Fame and Museum
Cooperstown, New York 13326

Basketball Hall of Fame
460 Alden Street
Springfield, Massachusetts 01109

Pro Football's Hall of Fame
Canton, Ohio 44708

Hockey Hall of Fame
Canadian National Exhibition Park
Toronto, Canada

Many collectors who specialize in the autographs of members of Baseball's Hall of Fame ask each individual to sign his "plaque card," the post card depicting the player's Hall of Fame commemorative plaque. These post cards can be ordered by mail from the Hall of Fame. They cost 5¢ each.

Send the plaque card in an envelope to the player, enclosing a letter requesting that he sign the card, plus a self-addressed, stamped envelope. "This strategy works with a high degree of success," says one collector. "Even Joe DiMaggio, who was somewhat difficult to get to sign in person, will sign a Hall of Fame plaque card."

There are hundreds of collectors involved in buying, selling, and trading the autographs of sports celebrities. Among the best known are: John J. Smith (23653 Sunset Crossing Road, Diamond Bar, California 91765), William White (109-A Fourth Avenue, Broomall, Pennsylvania 19008), and Dicky Ow (220 Mt. Hermon Road, Santa Cruz, California, 95060).

Many collectors with this specialty advertise in the hobby newspapers, some of which were noted in the first chapter. Two publications specialize in the advertisements from those who deal especially in sports material. They are:

The Trader Speaks (c/o Daniel Dischley, 3 Pleasant Drive, Lake Ronkonkoma, New York 11779); one year, 12 issues, $6.00; sample copy, 50¢.

The Sports Trader (P. O. Box 909, Cupertino, California 95104) ; one year, 12 issues, $3.50; sample copy, 40¢.

No matter what type of autographs you collect—government officials or sports celebrities, ambassadors or astronauts—keep a careful record of the letters of request you send out. People who ignore your first letter should be written to a second time.

Do your record-keeping in a loose-leaf notebook, devoting a separate lined page to each person you write. A typical notebook page might contain these entries:

Name:
Address:
First Request Mailed:
Second Request Mailed:
Reply Received:
Description of Item Received:

Not only will your notebook serve as a guide as to when it's time to send out a follow-up letter, it will also be an inventory record of your collection.

Once you've acquired a number of autographs, you may begin to notice how some fall into categories. Many signatures bear a direct relationship to the profession of the signer.

For example, a person who writes his name with straight up-and-down strokes is likely to be an artist, architect, inventor, composer, or writer. "Stand-up strokes often indicate a mildly introverted person," says graphologist George Reynolds, "a person who prefers working by himself or at least with a limited number of people."

A person whose signature slants to the right is likely to be more extroverted, Mr. Reynolds says. Business executives and almost all politicians fall into this category.

"The signature is an accurate clue to a person's emotional stance," Mr. Reynolds states. "It's a reflection of a role the person is playing."

4 *Fakery and Forgery*

P L I N Y   T H E   E L D E R , the Roman naturalist
and writer who died in the year 79 A.D., was known to collect
rare documents, which would mean that the collecting of autograph material has been flourishing for about two thousand
years. Through all of the hobby's long and rich history, collectors
and dealers have been plagued by the work of forgers. Not only
signatures, but letters, manuscripts, and documents of every
type have been falsely produced, often, unfortunately, with
great skill. Today, however, fakery and forgery are more wide-
spread than ever before. You're sure to face the problem once
you begin receiving signatures in the mail.

The more serious you are about collecting, the greater the
problem becomes. Autograph dealers look upon bogus signatures in much the same way a banker regards a counterfeit dollar
bill. First of all, it's terribly disheartening to come upon one.
Second, except for rare cases, it is absolutely worthless.

There are many different types of fake signatures. The printed
facsimile is the most common. These vary in type with the printing process used.

The signatures of the treasurer of the United States and the
secretary of the treasury that appear on our paper currency
result from an extremely sophisticated printing process, one

50

United States Senate

WASHINGTON, D.C.

May 19, 1965

Mr. George Sullivan
330 East 33rd Street
New York, New York

Dear Mr. Sullivan:

Thank you for your recent letter. Your views are most
helpful to me in carrying out my responsibilities as a United
States Senator representing the State of New York, and I
appreciate your having taken the time and effort to write to me.

Sincerely,

Robert F. Kennedy

Robert Kennedy's correspondence was often signed with an Autopen. This is one example.

that involves carefully etched plates and modern cylinder presses. Gum card "autographs" are also printed facsimiles. So are the signatures turned out by a mimeograph machine, a Xerox machine, or even a rubber stamp.

Because of the advances in printing technology in recent

years, it is sometimes difficult to distinguish a facsimile signature from one that is genuine. The first thing to look for are variations in color tone. An original signature will have gradations in color; a facsimile won't.

If the facsimile signature happens to be printed in black ink, it will be jet back from the first letter to the last; there will be no hint of gray. If the facsimile is printed in colored ink—blue, for instance—it will be a uniform shade of blue from beginning to end.

Also look for minute breaks in the script. Use a magnifying glass. Tiny gaps are sometimes common to facsimile signatures.

The reverse side of the page or photograph may also give a clue as to whether a signature is genuine. In the case of an original signature, you can often detect an impression created by the writing end of the pen. Facsimile printing leaves no such impression.

Printed facsimile signatures are almost wholly without value, but there are rare exceptions. During the Kennedy administration, boys and girls who wrote the president requesting an autograph received a small white card with the imprinted heading, "The White House," and below appeared the words, "With best wishes, John Kennedy." It was a facsimile signature, a fact the White House did not try to conceal. On its reverse side, the card stated: "This is an exact reproduction of the president's signature."

This admonition was scarcely necessary, for most people could tell at a glance that the signature was not genuine. Yet today these signature cards are listed in dealers' catalogs and priced as high as $10.00.

Some collectors, when they receive a facsimile signature, send it back to the person along with a polite note explaining that they collect only genuine autograph material. Then they ask for a "real" signature.

A more serious problem than facsimile signatures are those

With all best wishes,

Sincerely,

Richard Nixon

Richard Nixon

With every good wish,

Sincerely,

Richard Nixon

Richard Nixon

very best wishes.

Sincerely,

Richard Nixon

Richard Nixon

Richard Nixon

Experts have detected at least four different Richard Nixon Autopen signatures. (FROM THE COLLECTION OF A. CAVALLARO)

"written" by an Autopen, a robot device used by recent presidents, the astronauts, other top-level government officials, and business executives in signing correspondence and fulfilling autograph requests. Autopen signatures are as valueless as printed facsimiles but they are much more difficult to detect.

The Autopen Signature Machine, to use its full name, is manufactured by the International Autopen Company of Arlington, Virginia. It provides a true pen-and-ink reproduction of a

53

person's signature automatically and as many times as desired. The manufacturer describes the machine as "a fountain pen come to life."

The pen itself is mounted on a small table. The operator, a secretary or assistant, sits at the table, places the paper to be signed in the proper position, and presses down on a small foot pedal. The pen, following a plastic die, or "recording," of the person's signature, immediately whisks across the paper, producing a script that is indistinguishable from the original. The machine, which sold for $1,050.00 in 1970, can produce as many as three thousand signatures in an eight-hour day.

Writing machines such as the Autopen have a long history. The first was developed in Europe by Frederick von Knaus in 1753, and could actually write entire paragraphs of varying length and content. Later models of von Knaus' machine could even write out dictated messages. An operator seated at a keyboard simply punched out the appropriate letters.

While the concept of the Autopen is not new, its application certainly is. For centuries the device was looked upon as a mere toy, and mechanical writing instruments were exhibited at fairs and trade shows. But today the use of robot pens is pandemic. Autopens are used for signing letters, photographs, diplomas, checks, stock certificates, and all kinds of legal documents. Presidents Nixon, Johnson (and Lady Bird Johnson, too), and Kennedy, the late Senator Robert Kennedy, Senator Edward Kennedy, and New York's Governor Nelson Rockefeller are among those who have employed the Autopen.

"Both the American and Russian astronauts use automation to sign autographs for collectors," says dealer Charles Hamilton. "I once saw eight post card photographs of the first Russian spacewoman, all signed in pen and ink, but all identical!"

Sometimes the use of the Autopen can be detected by holding two examples of the same person's signature up to the light and superimposing one on the other. If they are Autopen signatures, they may match perfectly, right down to the slightest detail.

This method of detection can be thwarted, however, by a signer who employs several dies or engravings, each made from a different rendering of his signature. According to one source, President Kennedy's staff used an assortment of seven different robot patterns.

Not all Autopen signatures are without value. Some consideration has to be given to what is signed. For example, a document with meaningful content signed by the president would have value, even though the signature was of the Autopen variety.

Proxy signatures are yet another problem collectors must cope with. Proxy autographs refer to those signed by a secretary or assistant to the celebrity. Often they are called secretarial signatures.

Proxy signatures are extremely common to show business. If you write a television star or a well-known artist in the recording field, you are almost certain to receive a photograph of the personality bearing his pen-and-ink signature. But it's likely to have been dashed off by a secretary, a proxy.

The signature of the late President Kennedy was often produced by proxy. Dr. Milton Kronovet, a Brooklyn autograph dealer, was one of the first to recognize this fact. During the early 1960's, Dr. Kronovet accumulated hundreds of samples of Kennedy's signature. "In the case of letters signed by Kennedy," says Dr. Kronovet, "I began to notice that there was a close relationship between the signature and the secretarial initials that appeared in the lower left-hand corner of the page. When the initials were, say, 'c.b.,' Kennedy's signature had a certain character and form, but when the initials were 'j.r.,' the signature was entirely different. And each 'c.b.' signature resembled every other, and the same with every 'j.r.' signature. So it was obvious that Kennedy wasn't signing his letters, but his secretaries were signing for him."

Dealer Charles Hamilton has called John Kennedy's signature "one of the most baffling of modern times." After a thorough study of Kennedy's writing, Hamilton concluded that seven different Autopen signatures and fourteen different secretarial signatures were used in signing his name. Hamilton's findings are detailed in a book he write entitled, *The Robot That Helped to Make a President.*

How does one detect a proxy signature? It's not easy. Often the secretary who is authorized to sign for the person is extremely skilled in imitating the signature. This means that the collector or dealer has to have an intimate knowledge of what the individual's signature really looks like. Then through a comparison of signatures he may be able to distinguish the true from the false. It's a task for the expert.

Forged material is still another problem that collectors must be ready to face. This usually refers to signatures or documents that are falsely produced and claimed to be genuine.

Forged material is sometimes characterized by a "forced" look. The line edges may be wavy, and the script can have several different tonal qualities, caused by variations in stroke pressure. Sometimes there may be abrupt changes in the slant of the script or indications that the forger tried to patch or retrace his strokes.

Here are two samples of the signature of Button Gwinnett, one of the signers of the Declaration of Independence:

The bottom signature is a reproduction of the forgery. It shows clearly the forger's inclination to patch up, to over-write. There's attention to detail not typical of writing that is genuine. It is this elaborate effort to make the name look perfect that often distinguishes the real signature from the forgery, says *Manuscripts*.

If you are dubious about any item of autograph material, seek out another sample of the handwriting for the purpose of noting similarities and differences. Your local library is likely to have available facsimile signatures which you can use in making a comparison. Ask for a copy of the *Handbook of Facsimiles of Famous Personages* by Charles Geigy. The best known book of its type, it contains the printed signatures of more than 1,200 of the world's most notable figures of the past.

Besides the chance of buying forged material, there is also the hazard of buying stolen material. Thefts of important material from library collections and other institutions, while not frequent, do occur. If you don't happen to be buying from an established dealer, be sure you know where the seller obtained the material, particularly if it is an important document.

The best way to avoid buying stolen or forged material is to always make it a practice of dealing with a reputable person when you buy.

When you buy from a well-known dealer, he will guarantee

PASCAL, Blaise
1623—1662
illustre mathématicien - der berühmte Gelehrte - illustrious savant

CASSINI, Giov. Dom.
1625—1712
astronome italien
italienischer Astronom
Italian astronomer

HUYGENS, Christian
1629—1695
inventeur de la pendule
Erfinder der Penduluhr
inventor of the pendulum

SPINOZA, Baruch
1632—1677
grand philosophe hollandais
der grosse holländische Philosoph
great Dutch philosopher

NEWTON, Isaac
1642—1727
découvrit les lois de la gravitation universelle
Entdecker des Gravitationsgesetzes
discoverer of the law of gravitation

A typical page from Geigy's Handbook of Facsimiles of Famous Personages.

your purchase to be genuine. Should you later find the material to be spurious, the dealer will refund your money. Your bill of sale is likely to spell out this guarantee. This is your best safeguard against the chance of being defrauded.

58

5 Receiving Meaningful Replies

ADVANCED COLLECTORS and autograph dealers have little or no regard for mere signatures or signed photographs, except for an occasional rarity. Dealer Charles Hamilton calls such material ". . . mere scraps of evidence that a celebrity knows how to write his name."

It's true—signatures are of secondary importance as far as dollar value is concerned.

As you become more serious about collecting, you should seek to obtain material that is much more meaningful than the stereotyped items sent out by celebrities in answer to conventional letters of request. Of course, there's a certain delight in receiving a signature or a signed photograph, but, if you work at it, it is possible to obtain through the mail material that has real significance and important dollar value, material that is absolutely thrilling to receive.

A surprising number of the world's celebrities will correspond with you, once they are convinced that you are seriously interested in them or in the field that they represent. "There are two classes of autograph collectors," novelist Marjorie Kinnan Rawlings once commented. "There are those who own books that they care for and to whom the signature of an author means something; and half-witted little pests.

Mr. Herman M. Darvick
3109 Brighton 7th Street
Brooklyn, New York 11235

Dear Mr. Darvick:

I can go along with you on the ticket of Rockefeller and
Reagan. However, I personally favor Governor Romney.

The Republicans have an opportunity parallel in the last
thirty-six years only to that of 1952. We have yet to
demonstrate our ability to take advantage of that. It all
depends on the course of the convention and the course of
the campaign that the nominee makes.

I think we have a good chance of winning with anyone but
Nixon. His nomination will be a disaster for the
Republican Party.

              With every good wish -

AML:j

*Alf M. Landon, defeated by Franklin D. Roosevelt in the presidential
election of 1936, often corresponds with collectors.* (FROM THE COLLEC-
TION OF HERMAN DARVICK)

"The latter deserve no consideration except when they enclose a stamped self-addressed envelope." Then she added: "No
trouble is too great to accommodate the former."

As mentioned earlier, there is no need to have your letters
typed. "Handwritten letters are personal and imply sincerity,"
says an officer of the Universal Collectors Club. "They're every

bit as effective as a typewritten letter, perhaps even more so.

"And there is always the chance that the person you're writing to will be encouraged to write you a handwritten letter in return. You will thus have a more valuable item than if you were sent a typewritten letter."

Always print your name and address at the bottom of the letter as well as on the return envelope. If you enclose an item to be signed—a typewritten copy of a speech, for example— print your name and address in soft pencil on the reverse side. Sometimes the letter gets separated from the enclosure. Be sure to remember to enclose a stamped, self-addressed envelope or stamps to cover the cost of return postage.

Use first class mail, of course. Occasionally collectors register their letters. "This attracts attention to your letter," one collector explains. "It separates it from all the other mail the celebrity is getting, and boosts your rate of response."

When registering their letters, some collectors request a return receipt, because sometimes the celebrity signs that. They end up getting two autographs for one letter. Of course, registering letters adds to your expense.

Again, use matching paper and envelopes. Some collectors purchase letterhead stationery. To imprint 250 sheets of good quality stationery, $5\frac{1}{2}''$ x $8\frac{1}{2}''$ in size, white, with your name and address, will cost you between ten and fifteen dollars. Imprinted envelopes to match cost about the same. However, it is relatively unimportant whether you have specially printed stationery. What is important is your letter and what it says.

"The secret of building up a good autograph collection is in thinking," says Herman Darvick, president of the Universal Autograph Collectors Club. "It involves thinking up intelligent and comment-provoking letters.

"You have to be creative about it. Really work on your letter, plan its content, and you're likely to be rewarded with a dazzling reply."

The Star-Spangled Banner.

O say! can you see by the dawn's early light
What so proudly we hail'd at the twilight's last gleaming
Whose broad stripes and bright stars, through the clouds of the fight,
O'er the ramparts we watch'd were so gallantly streaming!
And the rocket's red glare - the bomb bursting in air
Gave proof through the night that our flag was still there !
O say, does that star-spangled banner yet wave
O'er the land of the free & the home of the brave? —

F S Key

Francis Scott Key responded to a collector's request for a handwritten copy of the words to "The Star-Spangled Banner." Today, the document is worth $50,000.

You have to become as knowledgeable as you can about the person you're writing to. Study his biography in one of the suggested reference books. Become familiar with his achievements. Really get to know the person before you sit down to write.

"Forget that you want an autograph when you write," says Dr. Milton Kronovet. "Your chief interest should be in the person, in his career."

Don't try to turn out letters in great volume. Instead, plan a campaign of long duration, writing only one or two a week. Your goal should be to make each letter thoughtful and meaningful, rather than to dash off a great many that are ordinary and spiritless.

There is an endless list of people you can write to—artists and authors, scientists and surgeons, concert singers and civil rights leaders. The names and addresses of more than one hundred celebrities are listed in the appendix of this book. For additional names, consult the reference books noted earlier.

When you write, it is often a good idea to ask the person a question, one that will take only a few moments of his time to answer. You might ask a noted author what is his favorite book of those he has written, or you might ask an artist to name his favorite painting.

A Barrington, New Jersey, collector, who has gathered over five thousand autographs in response to letters he has sent out, often writes to government officials or persons prominent in political life, and asks this question: "What is your definition of a great American?"

Many collectors ask topical questions. The nation's court system is beseiged with problems, and in many parts of the country court calendars are congested, the poor are inadequately represented, and sometimes minor criminal cases are handled in careless fashion. A letter to a justice of the Supreme Court might ask for a comment on one of these problems, or an opinion on how a specific problem might be solved. Make the letter personal and original, drawing examples from the court system in your own area.

A collector's letter to former British Prime Minister Clement Attlee asked, "What was the greatest contribution made by Prime Minister Churchill in the cause of world peace?"

It evoked a brief but colorful reply. "Dear Sir," said Attlee, "Sir Winston's greatest service to world peace was in leading the defeat of Hitler, the Nazi gangster."

Do your homework carefully. You can never tell what an intelligently written letter will lead to. Some years ago, dealer-collector Paul C. Richards was assigned by his college professor to write a paper to be entitled "Henry A. Wallace and the Progressive Party in 1948." Mr. Wallace, who had served as United States vice-president, secretary of agriculture, and secretary of commerce, was living in retirement on his farm at South Salem, New York, and Mr. Richards wrote to him requesting

THE GOOD EARTH
Chapter One

Pearl S. T Buck

It was Wang Lung's marriage day. At first, opening his eyes in the blackness of the curtains about his bed, he could not think why the dawn seemed different from any other. The house was still except for the faint, gasping cough of his old father, whose room was opposite to his own across the middle room. Every morning the old man's cough was the first sound to be heard. Wang Lung usually lay listening to it and moved only when he heard it approaching nearer and when he heard the door of his father's room squeak upon its wooden hinges.

But this morning he did not wait. He sprang up and pushed aside the curtains of his bed. It was a dark, ruddy dawn, and through a small square hole of a window, where the tattered paper fluttered, a glimpse of bronze sky gleamed. He went to the hole and tore the paper away.

Pearl Buck's signature on a typescript of the first page of The Good Earth *is a meaningful addition to any collection.*

information. Mr. Wallace responded with a letter rich in detail and also sent printed material concerning his unsuccessful try for the presidency.

The two began an almost weekly exchange of letters, and out of this developed a friendship that lasted until Mr. Wallace's death in 1965. In their correspondence, Mr. Wallace discussed his association with Franklin D. Roosevelt and other New Deal leaders, his career as a political servant, his involvement with the Progressive Party, and his experimental work in agriculture. He gave Mr. Richards many handwritten copies of speeches and letters, two authentically signed letters from President Kennedy, and he wrote a letter of introduction to President Harry S Truman on Mr. Richards' behalf.

As Mr. Richards' experience suggests, many government officials and political figures who have returned to private life enjoy corresponding with collectors who are sincere in their interest. Alf M. Landon, defeated by Franklin D. Roosevelt in the presidential election of 1936, lives in retirement in Kansas City, and writes letters filled with provocative comment about the period in which he was in the public eye. Dean Acheson corresponds with those who show an interest in the problems he faced as secretary of state from 1949-1953. A Belleville, New

Jersey, collector writes to and receives letters regularly from former Vice-President Hubert Humphrey.

Letters that you receive from personalities are yours to keep, destroy, give away, read aloud before your friends or relatives (not on television or radio), or sell. You can do all of these without the writer's permission. However, the writer of the letter retains certain ownership rights and you should be aware of them.

The contents of the letter belongs to the writer. He owns the literary rights. This means that you cannot copy the letter or allow it to be published, in whole or in part, without the consent of the writer.

Suppose you received a letter from novelist Norman Mailer containing incisive comments about the American literary scene. The editor of your local newspaper might wish to reproduce the letter or quote from it. In either case, you would first have to obtain Mr. Mailer's permission.

But suppose Mr. Mailer wanted to publish the contents of the letter, perhaps as part of a magazine article. Could he do so without your permission? Indeed, he could. He owns the con-

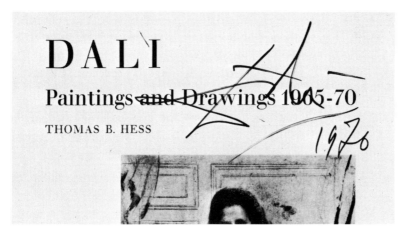

This is worthwhile, too: Salvador Dali's signature on the cover of an exhibition catalog.

tents; he can do with them as he wishes. Your consent is not necessary.

Early in 1951, Barbara Heggie wrote an article in a national women's magazine that concerned the social and personal difficulties sometimes encountered by members of the family of the president. The article was called "What Makes Margaret Sing," a reference to Margaret Truman, the daughter of President Harry Truman, who was in office at the time the article was written.

Not long after the article appeared, the president wrote a warm and personal letter to Miss Heggie in which he thanked her for the article. "The vast majority of our people," said Mr. Truman, "can never understand what a terrible handicap it is to a lovely girl to have her Father the President of the United States."

Miss Heggie wrote to the president and asked permission to publish the letter. Mr. Truman refused, saying that the letter was "a personal matter between you and me . . ." and indicating he was afraid that it would appear that he had written the letter for the purpose of publication.

Miss Heggie made a second request. Again, Mr. Truman refused.

Miss Heggie then sold the letter to a dealer, and later it became the property of Richard Maass, then the president of The Manuscript Society. Late in 1954, after Mr. Truman had left office, Mr. Maass wrote to him and asked if he might allow a friend who was writing a book on the personal writings of the presidents to publish the letter. This time Mr. Truman agreed.

To sum up, you own the physical property, the paper and ink, of any letter you receive. The writer owns what the letter says.

The only exception to these legal restrictions occurs in the case of a letter written by a government official acting in an official capacity. In this instance, the letter becomes a public

FIRST DAY OF ISSUE

NASA
ATLAS-MERCURY
AT LIFT OFF

FEB 20
3 30PM
1962
FLA.

FIRST DAY OF ISSUE

PROJECT MERCURY

COMMEMORATING
FIRST SUCCESSFUL ORBITAL FLIGHT
BY AN AMERICAN · FEB 20, 1962
JOHN H. GLENN, JR.

A good number of collectors specialize in signed first-day covers.

document and can be reproduced or published without the writer's authorization.

Occasionally one of your letters may bring forth a document of great value. Lewis J. Cist, an autograph collector of the mid-nineteenth century, specialized in collecting poems in the handwriting of the authors. Cist wrote to Francis Scott Key and requested a handwritten copy of the words to "The Star-Spangled Banner." Key obliged. Charles Hamilton, in his book, *Scribblers and Scoundrels*, estimates that today this document is worth "at least $50,000." And all it cost Cist was a three-cent stamp.

Besides letters, there are many other forms of colorful material you can obtain from the world's famous personages. You can ask an author to sign a typewritten transcript—called a "typescript"—of a page from one of his or her books or plays. You might have a composer autograph a page of sheet music of one of his compositions. Send the item to be signed, along with a polite letter of request and the postage to cover the return of the enclosed material.

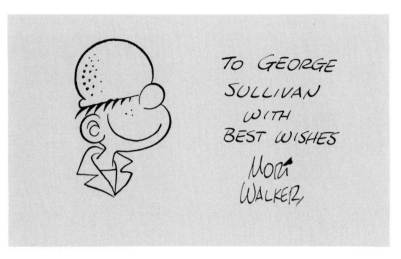

Some cartoonists answer autograph requests with inscribed cards like this one.

A good number of collectors specialize in signed first-day covers, envelopes bearing newly issued stamps which have been postmarked on the stamp's first day of issue. There is always an association between the subject of the cover and signer. For instance, one collector has architect Philip Johnson's signature on a cover bearing the stamp which honors the American Institute of Architects. A New York dealer recently offered an "ornate first-day American Music cover," which was signed by composers Ira Gershwin and Irving Berlin. Astronaut signatures on first-day covers commemorating space achievements are extremely popular among young collectors.

Other collectors seek autographed books. "I have sent out over two hundred books for autographing all over the world," says Robert Notlep in his book, *The Autograph Collector*, "and have never had a request refused."

Send the book to the author with a letter requesting that he inscribe the book to you. Express an interest in the book or the subject matter.

To mail the book, use a special "book mailer," a heavily

padded envelope. Simply insert the book, plus a book mailer to be used for the return mailing. Also enclose your letter. Fold over the top of the bag and secure it with staples or tape. Book mailers, which can be purchased at stationery stores, are not expensive. A dozen, 8″ x 12″ in size, costs less than $2.50.

Write the words "Book—Special Fourth Class Rate" on the outside of the mailing bag. This special rate is considerably less than the first-class postal rate, and even less than parcel post service. Seldom will it cost you more than twenty-four cents to mail a book, as long as it is not going overseas. Also write the words "First Class Letter Enclosed" on the outside of the book mailer, and affix an extra first class stamp.

While it does not cost a great deal to mail books, the service is far from speedy. Prepare to wait several weeks for your book to return.

The nation's cartoonists, both the editorial cartoonists and

GROSSADMIRAL a. D. DÖNITZ

dankt für die guten Wünsche zum Weihnachtsfest

und zum neuen Jahr und erwidert sie herzlich.

Grand Admiral Doenitz, Supreme Commander of the German military forces during World War II, often responds to greeting cards with "Hearty greetings" and a signature. (FROM THE COLLECTION OF WILLIAM J. SULLIVAN)

The New York Times

LATE CITY EDITION
Weather: Rain, warm today; clear tonight. Sunny, pleasant tomorrow. Temp. range: today 80-86; Sunday 71-66. Temp.-Hum. Index yesterday 69. Complete U.S. report on P. 55.

VOL. CXVIII...No. 40,721   © 1969 The New York Times Company.   NEW YORK, MONDAY, JULY 21, 1969   10 CENTS

MEN WALK ON MOON

ASTRONAUTS LAND ON PLAIN; COLLECT ROCKS, PLANT FLAG

Astronaut Edwin E. (Buzz) Aldrin was asked to sign this newspaper headline for a collector—and did.

those who draw the comic strips, are a source of extremely colorful autograph material. The noted Charles Schulz sometimes sends out his signature in an envelope adorned with the well-known drawing of Snoopy in repose atop his doghouse. Other cartoonists often respond with an original drawing of their leading characters.

If you send your favorite cartoonist a panel of his cartoon from your local newspaper and ask him to autograph it for you, he is likely to do so. Sometimes cartoonists honor requests for autographed samples of their preliminary pen-and-ink sketches.

In writing a cartoonist, what do you use for an envelope address? His "syndicate"—the name of the agency that sells and distributes the strip. The name of the syndicate, in very small type, always appears somewhere within the cartoon feature.

Three of the largest cartoon syndicates are King Features Syndicate (235 East 45th Street, New York, New York 10017); United Features Syndicate (220 East 42nd Street, New York, New York 10017), and the Chicago Tribune-New York News Syndicate (22 East 42nd Street, New York, New York 10017). If the syndicate you want to write to is not one of these, call your local newspaper and ask for the address.

Or, at your local library, consult a copy of the *Editor & Publisher Syndicate Directory*. This publication lists every

70

comic strip and cartoon, from "Abie an' Slats" to "Yogi Bear," more than three hundred of them, along with the name of the artist for each and the syndicate address. You can obtain a copy of this publication by writing Circulation Department, *Editor & Publisher* (850 Third Avenue, New York, New York 10022). The directory costs $2.00.

Countless advanced collectors specialize in autographed photographs, but not the commonplace photographs sent out by television personalities or baseball players. Instead, they obtain photographs that depict significant events, and then have them signed by the person or persons involved in the event.

For example, a Canton, Ohio, collector was successful in having Ambassador Averell Harriman sign a photograph that represented the peace talks in Paris in which Harriman participated and which were meant to bring an end to the war in Viet Nam. Another collector had trackman John Carlos sign a photograph taken as he gave the Black Power salute at the Olympic medal

Commander Lloyd Bucher's signature appears on a photograph of the U.S.S. Pueblo, *the ship he commanded which was captured by the North Koreans.*

Vote for New York.

Committee To Elect The Lindsay Team, 41 E. 45th St., N. Y., N. Y. 10017 · Harvard Offset Company, Inc., 621 Avenue of the Americas, N.Y., N.Y. 10011

Lindsay, Perrotta, Garelik

New York's Mayor John V. Lindsay is cooperative in granting autographs. Here his signature appears on a campaign poster.

ceremony in Mexico City in 1968. Each day brings news events which trigger exciting photographs involving prominent people. Simply scan your daily newspaper for ideas.

When you see a photograph you want, look for the credit line. It's the tip-off as to where the photograph can be obtained. The great bulk of the nation's newspaper photographs are sent out by either the Associated Press (Wide World Photos, 50 Rockefeller Plaza, New York, New York 10020) or United Press (22 East 42nd Street, New York, New York 10017).

In either case, write to the news agency and request an 8″ x 10″ glossy print of the photograph you want. Explain that you want the photograph for your personal use and that you are not planning to have it published. The Associated Press charges $7.50 for each picture; United Press International charges $5.00. Enclose a check with your order.

The various executive departments and independent agencies of the federal government are an excellent source of photographs, and the prices involved are considerably less than when dealing with a private news agency. The Photographic Agency of the United States Army (Department of Defense, The Pentagon, Washington, D. C., 20310), the Photographic Records Division of the National Archives (Pennsylvania Avenue at 8th Street, N. W., Washington, D. C., 20004), the National Aeronautics and Space Administration, the Library of Congress, the Smithsonian Institution, the Department of Transportation, the Department of Agriculture—all of these and many others have available photographs in the greatest abundance.

When ordering, give complete details as to the particular photograph you want. In return, you are likely to receive an order form describing what is available and indicating prices. Photographs from government agencies usually cost about one dollar each. Payment must be made in advance.

The late Reverend Cornelius Greenway of Brooklyn, one of the most noted collectors of recent times, specialized in autographed photographs. He would visit a news agency and purchase a photograph of a well-known figure in a dramatic scene, then send the picture to the celebrity with a note, encouraging the individual to sign the picture and to write a comment concerning the depicted incident.

In time, he built a collection that included virtually every single one of the world's great leaders. But one kept eluding his efforts—Nikita Khrushchev, the Russian premier. After several abortive attempts, the Reverend Greenway hit upon the idea of sending Khrushchev a picture of the first Russian moon strike, an event in which the Russians took immense pride. It worked!

Office of the White House Press Secretary

THE WHITE HOUSE

THE WHITE HOUSE MADE PUBLIC TODAY
THE FOLLOWING LETTER FROM THE
PRESIDENT TO THE PRESIDENT OF THE
SENATE AND THE SPEAKER OF THE HOUSE
OF REPRESENTATIVES

February 25, 1965

Dear Mr. President: (Dear Mr. Speaker:)

It is my pleasure to transmit legislation to authorize the appropriation
of $125.2 million for the Peace Corps in Fiscal Year 1966.

The Peace Corps will, in a few days, reach its fourth anniversary.
Since its beginning, on March 1, 1961, the Peace Corps has justified
the highest hopes of those who established it. The Congress intended
that this new agency would help peoples of interested countries and
areas "in meeting their needs for trained manpower, and to help promote
a better understanding of the American people on the part of the peoples
served and a better understanding of other peoples on the part of the
American people. "

Former President Lyndon Johnson signed this document for the author.

Back came the photograph with a large bold signature affixed.

Christmas, New Year's, and other holidays offer you a splendid opportunity to add to your collection of colorful unusual
autograph material. Many of the world's notables and government leaders respond to holiday greeting cards with handwritten expressions of gratitude. Or a letter of congratulations to a
head of state in connection with his country's national holiday
often evokes a handwritten response. The national holidays for
most countries are given in the booklet, *Permanent Missions to
the United Nations*, referred to earlier.

As an advanced collector, rely on your imagination. Don't
allow yourself to be satisfied with routine material. You should
seek out autograph items that have greater significance than
mere signatures or signed photographs.

The cost involved for stationery and postage stamps is exactly
the same as when you write a recording star or a football quarterback. The only difference is in the amount of original thinking you put forth.

74

6 Buying from Dealers

SERIOUS COLLECTING involves buying material from one or several of the nation's forty or so autograph dealers. It's the same in the case of stamps, coins, and most other collectible items.

Suppose you wanted to build up a worthwhile stamp collection, one that would have important value in the years to come. Experts say that the first thing you should do is to pick out a country in which to specialize. Then get to know as much as you possibly can about the stamps issued by that country and their relative values. You do this by reading stamp catalogs and publications about stamps, and by consulting stamp dealers and reading their catalog listings. The shrewd collector seeks to buy issues that he feels are going to be scarce in the future and that are currently underpriced.

Autograph collecting is the same in many ways. First, decide upon your specialty. The next step is to become fully informed about your field. Only when you're armed with knowledge can you make intelligent buying decisions.

As a teen-ager, Paul C. Richards, now a Brookline, Massachusetts, dealer, collected letters, documents, and signatures of persons prominent in all walks of life. "But the need to specialize soon became apparent," he says, "because it was financially impossible to collect simultaneously in all fields."

After giving the matter considerable thought, he decided to concentrate on the letters and documents of Edward Everett. Well known as an orator and writer, Everett, who died in 1865, had a distinguished career in public life. He served as governor of Massachusetts, president of Harvard, ambassador to England, secretary of state, and was a candidate for vice-president.

Two factors contributed to Mr. Richards' decision. "First," he says, "there appeared to be an abundant amount of Everett material on the market, thus indicating his autographs were not being currently collected. Second, the available material was modestly priced, and, in fact, I felt was too modest in price for the importance of the man."

After making his choice, Mr. Richards visited a noted dealer —Gordon Banks of Goodspeed's in Boston—and asked to see what was available on Everett. From a bulging folder, Mr. Richards selected an assortment of Everett letters and the handwritten manuscript of a Fourth of July address. He paid seventy-five dollars for the material—"eagerly" he recalls—and his collection was launched. He then wrote other dealers advising them of his interest in Everett material.

Later, Mr. Richards expanded his collecting activities. He became interested in the poet Robert Frost, and today his collection of Frost's letters, manuscripts, and books is one of the largest still in private hands. In more recent years, Mr. Richards began collecting the letters, manuscripts, and books of Henry A. Wallace, United States agriculturist, author, and vice-president from 1941 to 1945, and of Theodore Roosevelt. Mr. Richards says that he decided to specialize in Roosevelt because "I wanted to collect a colorful individual from a past era."

Mr. Richards advises the person with only a moderate amount of capital to specialize in collecting the letters and documents of a person who has been neglected by libraries and other institutions. "This type of material is generally quite modest in price," he says, "and yet can convey the excitement and pleasure of collecting.

Andrew:

London
24 March 1779.

I have nothing more to say
as to Andrew Dalrymple's debt than
before. After shillings in the pound be
not paid he must be imprisoned if he
can be found. If he leaves the country
I cannot prevent it

William Samson's Account
must be paid. I hope it will not again
be so large.

I am glad to see that you atten
well to my plantations. By all means
let the oaks on Willockstown brae
be dressed, and any thing else done
that is necessary.

I hope care is taken that the
hair fowls go to Mr Bruce Campbell
when he wants them

I shall make inquiry as to the
subject of Gavin Lambie's letter.

I am your sincere friend
James Boswell

*This is an A.L.S. (autograph letter signed)—a letter in the handwriting
of the author—here, James Boswell—and signed by him.*

This is an A.D.S. (autograph document signed)—a document in the handwriting of the author and signed by him. The document is one recommending the passage of a bill by the New York state legislature, written and signed by New York's Governor George Clinton in 1795.
(FROM THE COLLECTION OF HERMAN DARVICK)

"The vice-presidents and cabinet officers are good groups to collect," continues Mr. Richards. "Prime ministers of England have been another sadly neglected field. Certain composers and performers can be obtained at low cost."

78

Many people believe that dealers offer only material that sells for many hundreds of dollars. Not at all. They do sell items and lots for hundreds of dollars, indeed, for thousands of dollars, but there is an enormous amount of material available for very modest sums.

For five dollars, you can purchase such items as: a photograph signed by German statesman Willy Brandt; the signature of Hugh McCulloch, secretary of the treasury in Lincoln's cabinet; a photograph signed by American actress Gloria Swanson; or a short note signed by Carlos Romulo, ambassador from the Philippines to the United Nations.

For between five and ten dollars, you can buy: a letter handwritten and signed by World War II General Omar Bradley; a card signed by Civil War General William Tecumseh Sherman; the signature of American explorer Richard E. Byrd, or a first-day cover honoring the inauguration of Luis Muñoz Marín, first elected governor of Puerto Rico, and signed by him.

After you've determined your field of specialty and done some studying about it, write to several dealers and request a catalog from each. Most dealers do not charge for catalogs.

When you write, it's a good idea to indicate your field of interest. Your request will be taken more seriously. Also, tell the dealer how much you wish to spend. Some dealers specialize in low-priced material, others in expensive items, and still others in material at every price level. What you want to do is establish a relationship with only those dealers whose offerings match your budget.

The more the dealer knows about your needs, the better able he is to help you. When you wish to purchase a specific item, give the dealer a detailed description of what you want. It isn't sufficient to say something like this: "I want to buy a Franklin Roosevelt letter. How much does one cost?"

It's impossible for a dealer to answer this kind of question. Do you want a handwritten letter or merely a typewritten one?

Do you want a letter signed while Roosevelt was in office or before he became president? Do you want a personal letter or one referring to a matter of government? How long should the letter be? These are only a few of the questions your description must answer.

The same is true when selling a letter. "I have a letter signed by Harry Truman. How much is it worth?" Dealers get asked questions like this all the time, but in nine cases out of ten, the dealer must personally examine the item being offered before he can supply the answer. He wants to appraise its condition, learn what it says, and weigh all the other factors that go toward establishing value.

A dealer can be helpful to you in many ways. "Bear in mind that unless you are an experienced collector in a narrow field, the dealer has probably seen more material than you ever will," Howard S. Mott, a Sheffield, Massachusetts, dealer points out. "An active dealer buys and sells more autographs in a year than most collectors see in a lifetime."

This knowledge and experience enables an active dealer to give you wise counsel concerning the field in which you specialize. He will be able to tell exactly what kind of material is available in the field and give you general information as to prevailing prices.

Dealers are also helpful in establishing the authenticity of an item. A dealer can detect an Autopen signature in an instant. "You get a feeling for what's authentic," says Dr. Milton Kronovet, a Brooklyn dealer. "You get so you can pick out an Autopen signature as easily as the average person can spot a five dollar bill in a handful of ones."

Most dealers prepare their catalog listings with the greatest diligence. Their motive is to give you, the prospective buyer, an exact picture in words of each item being offered. Descriptions are wholly honest. They mention the bad points—stains, tears, or other damage—as well as the good.

80

MEMORANDUM OF AN AGREEMENT

MADE THIS TWENTY FIFTH DAY OF APRIL ONE THOUSAND EIGHT HUNDRED AND SEVENTY SEVEN BETWEEN THOMAS HARDY ESQ OF STURMINSTER NEWTON, BLANDFORD OF THE ONE PART AND MESSRS HENRY S.KING & CO LONDON PUBLISHERS OF THE OTHER PART.

MR HARDY IS NOW THE OWNER OF THE COPYRIGHT OF THE STORY WRITTEN BY HIM ENTITLED "A PAIR OF BLUE EYES" AND HE HEREBY ASSIGNS THE SAME TO MESSRS HENRY S.KING & CO FOR THE PERIOD OF FIVE YEARS FROM THE FIRST DAY OF JUNE NOW NEXT ENSUING.

MESSRS HENRY S.KING & CO IN CONSIDERATION THEREOF AGREE TO REPRINT AND PUBLISH THE SAME AND TO PAY TO MR THOMAS HARDY TWO THIRDS OF THE PROFIT THAT MAY BE DERIVED FROM SUCH PUBLICATION DURING THE SAID PERIOD.

AND IT IS UNDERSTOOD THAT ALL DETAILS CONNECTED WITH THE SAID PUBLICATION SHALL BE IN THE CONTROL OF MESSRS HENRY S.KING & CO.

Thomas Hardy.

Here is a D.S. (document signed). English novelist and poet Thomas Hardy is the signer.

The first piece of information in a catalog listing is usually the name of the author of the item. This is followed by a few words of descriptive information about the person. For example:

CAGNEY, JAMES. American actor.

EDDY, MARY BAKER (1821-1910). Founder of the Christian Science Church.

FULTON, ROBERT (1765-1815). American artist, civil engineer, and inventor. Pioneer in steam navigation. His *Clermont* was the first commercially profitable steamboat ever built.

This information is followed by a description of the item it-

> *Fair Lady – had I but the time*
> *I'd give a touch of the sublime.*
> *But Wit – when summon'd at my call*
> *Seldom if ever comes at all*
> *If on this page you cast your eye*
> *And find it dull, and flat, and dry,*
> *Turn to the next and you shall find*
> *Bright emanations of the mind:*
> *And streams of choicest wisdom draw*
> *Deep from the fountains of the Law.*
>
> $\qquad\qquad$ *John Quincy Adams*
>
> *Washington 12 March 1842*

Here is an example of an A.Ms.S (autograph manuscript signed)—a poem written by and in the hand of President John Quincy Adams and signed by him.

self. Usually the item is designated as a letter, note, document, quotation, or manuscript. Dealers and collectors have very specific meanings in mind when they use these words.

A letter is a piece of personal correspondence, any communication that begins with a saluation and ends with the writer's signature. It can be a single sheet, five pages, fifty pages—any length. In catalogs, L is the abbreviation for letter.

A note is a brief written comment or communication. It does

not have a saluation. N is the catalog abbreviation for a note.

A document is a legal or official paper, such as a deed, military discharge, a will, or even a presidential proclamation. It can also be a telegram or a bank check. D is the abbreviation for document.

The term quotation can refer to the lines of a poem or a sentence or passage from a book. Q is abbreviation for quotation.

A manuscript is the material for a book, speech, poem, or play in either written or typewritten form. Ms. is the abbreviation for manuscript.

The word "holograph" is sometimes used to describe manuscript material written entirely in the handwriting of the author. A cut signature is a signature cut from a letter or document.

The catalog listing also specifies in what form the item appears and whether it is signed. A, for autograph, is used to indicate that an item appears in the handwriting of the author. S means that the item has been signed by the author.

These abbreviations are used in various combinations. Here

This is an A.Q.S. (autograph quotation signed). It is a passage handwritten by American poet Walt Whitman and signed by him.

are the ones you'll encounter most often:

A.L.S. (autograph letter signed)—a letter in the handwriting of the author and signed by him.

L.S. (letter signed)—usually a typewritten letter, and one that bears the signature of the author. The abbreviation T is used in some catalogs to indicate a letter that is typewritten, and T.L.S. is a signed typewritten letter.

A.D.S. (autograph document signed)—a document in the handwriting of the author and signed by him.

D.S. (document signed)—usually a printed document, and one signed by the author.

A.Ms.S. (autograph manuscript signed)—a handwritten manuscript that has been signed by the author.

A.Q.S. (autograph quotation signed)—a handwritten passage signed by the author.

Q.S. (quotation signed)—a typewritten or printed passage signed by the author.

The catalog description also covers the physical characteristics of the item being offered. Its size, for one thing. Often material is described as being folio size, abbreviated *fol.* A folio is a sheet approximately 12″ x 16″.

Quarto, abbreviated *4to*, is another size designation. It refers to a sheet that is approximately 8″ x 12″ in size. Other terms used to describe the physical dimensions of an item are:

octavo (8vo)—6″ x 8″ (approx.)
duodecimo (12mo)—3″ x 4″ (approx.)
sextodecimo (16mo)—1″ x 2″ (approx.)

If the document's length surpasses its width, it will be described as *oblong*, which is abbreviated *obl.*

The abbreviation *p* indicates *page*, and *pp.* is *pages*. The abbreviation *7pp.* means seven pages. But it does not mean seven sheets. When a sheet is written on both sides, each one is considered a page. So 7pp. would mean that there are four sheets,

84

three written on both sides, and one written on one side.

Certain punctuation marks in dealers' catalogs have special meaning, too. Parentheses around a person's name in a catalog indicate that the individual did not write or sign the item; the material merely refers to him in some way.

Brackets surrounding a date—[1876], for example—indicate that the author or signer did not affix a date to the manuscript material. The bracketed date is one that researchers have assigned to the document.

Other abbreviations you may see in catalog listings include:

g.e.	gilt-edged	sgd.	signed
mtd.	mounted	sm.	small
n.d.	no date	sq.	square
n.p.	no place	trans.	translation
n.y.	no year	v.d.	various dates
port.	portrait	vol.	volume
ptd.	printed	w. env.	with envelope
sign.	signature	wm.	watermark

The length and eloquence of catalog descriptions cover a wide range.

Inexpensive items are described in brief:

FIELDS, GRACIE. Entertainer. Attractive signed postcard photograph. 7.50

FRIEDMAN, IGNAZ. 1882-1948. Polish pianist and composer. Autograph Musical Quotation Signed. 1p., 8vo. New York, 1922. With a holograph comment re the music. 15.00

FARMER, JAMES. Negro leader; former head of C.O.R.E. Ornate cacheted First Day Cover marking the 175th Anniversary of the Bill of Rights. 1966. Signed by Farmer. 7.50

FURTWANGLER, WILHELM. German conductor. Autograph Letter Signed, in German. 1 full p., 4to. Berlin, Jan. 3, 1931. Musical content, mentioning Bach. Scarce. 25.00

FARNOL, JEFFREY. English novelist. Attractive oblong postcard-size photograph showing Farnol seated. Boldly signed, inscribed and dated 1931, on light background. 10.00

FULLER, R. BUCKMINSTER. American architect. Attractive cacheted American First Day Cover, postmarked from the U.S. Pavilion, Expo 67, Montreal. The cachet shows the design for the U.S. Pavilion, which Fuller designed. Attractively signed. 15.00

Items of about average value are modestly described:

BALAKIREV, MILI. 1837-1910. Russian composer. Letter Signed, in German. 2 pp., 8vo. Petersburg, 1/14 April 1902. Apparently to a German publisher. Balakirev requests him to send the Concerto and the Ballad by Liapunov. "For ethical reasons" he wants to know whether these are successful "with you". The Ballad had been played with great success in Petersburg the previous year and in Prague in January. He offers the manuscript to his correspondent if he wishes to publish a four-hand edition. Rare. 125.00

MITCHELL, WILLIAM. American General; court martialed for his vigorous support of air power. Autograph Letter Signed, on his imprinted personal stationery. 4pp., 4to. Boxwood, Nov. 6, 1926. To James P. Pond, accepting a lecture date in Erie. He does not wish to undertake any more lectures unless they are close to him, and pay at least 500 dollars. But he considers the publicity for his lectures of equal importance. He continues: "I want to give a lecture on the Pacific question, as I have never before given a public one and one of this kind has never been given in America..." With an unsigned 4to photograph of Mitchell in uniform. Scarce autograph. 125.00

HANLEY, JAMES. English writer. Autograph Manuscript Signed of a chapter for Resurrexit Dominus. 14pp., 4to, together with the holograph dedication leaf from the author presenting the manuscript to the American poet and novelist Frederic Prokosch. With an A.L.S. from Hanley to Prokosch, dated Feb. 8 (1932). Privately issued in a very small edition in 1934, Resurrexit Dominus has never been published in a trade edition. The present manuscript is headed "Part Four", and contains two sensational episodes; that in which the Irish servant girl is accosted and, later, the "stroke" of her employer, Father Hooley. 150.00

Sometimes a description will include illustrative material:

GERSHWIN, GEORGE. American composer. Autograph Musical Quotation Signed from his Second Rhapsody. 1p., 8vo. Oct. 15, 1933. Inscribed to a member of the Boston Symphony Orchestra (name could be easily trimmed away). See illustration. 275.00

Really important material is described in rich detail:

EDWARDS, JONATHAN. 1703-1758. American Congregational clergyman and theologian; led celebrated religious revival. Autograph Letter Signed. 1 full p., 4to. Stockbridge, Mass., January 24, 1755. To Rev. Joseph Bellamy, pastor in Bethlehem, Connecticut. Addressed on verso. In 1754 Edwards had published his book on freedom of will, which "revealed him as the first great philosophical intelligence in American history" [D.A. B.]. This work, which is one of the Grolier Club's One Hundred Influential American Books Printed Before 1900, extended his reputation from the Colonies to Great Britain and Europe. The recipient of this letter , who was also a leading clergyman of his time, was a pupil, protege, and disciple of Edwards. Born in Cheshire, Conn., he was Yale 1735, and for many years pastor in Bethlehem. "He was full of enthusiasm for the Great Awakening, and for the New Light theology, inaugurated by...Edwards." D.A.B. The McGregore mentioned in Edwards's letter was probably the Rev. David McGregore, pastor in Londonderry, N.H. Edwards writes in part: "I am sorry you have put by your

Journey hither. I want to see you very much, & to have you bring the books. I must, if Providence allows, be at Windsor the week after the 20 of April to meet my sister... I am fully of your Mind about Mr. McGregore. I wonder I never thought of him before. I have sent along a number of Letters for you...one that came from Boston I guess has a Piece of Gold in it...." Of utmost rarity, being the first letter from this legendary Colonial preacher to pass through our hands. Handsomely preserved.   750.00

JACKSON, ANDREW. President and General. Magnificent Autograph Letter Signed. Nearly 2 full pp., legal folio. Washington City, April 15, 1824. Addressed simply "My Dear Wife." Affectionate family letter, from which space allows us to quote only in small part: "It is still uncertain when I can leave here. The Tariff bill is still under discussion, & has been reported to the House, & I hope the final vote will be taken on it on Saturday next. I hope...next week I will be able to say to you on what day I will be able to leave here. How grateful I am, for the health you continue to enjoy and how thankfull to the all ruling Providence for this blessing that he has bestowed upon you in my absence. I have my love said, & trust a kind providence will enable me to full-fill that after we meet again, we will not separate, that wherever I go, there shalt you go also, for I am sure if you were with me I could be contented....accept my prayers for your health & happiness until we have the pleasure of meeting. Yours affection-ately..." With handsome engraved portrait of Jackson. Really choice!   1000.00

These examples are from catalogs issued by Paul C. Richards. With other dealers, descriptions are much the same.

It's wise to read a dealer's catalog as soon as it arrives. If you come upon an item that interests you and is attractively priced, order it right away. Several hundred other people may receive the catalog, and delay diminishes the chances your order will be filled. Of course, the bargain-priced items go the quickest.

A few dealers will send you material on approval. This means that the items are returnable; you make your decision to purchase only after examining the material. Items not purchased must be returned at once. Policy varies somewhat from dealer to dealer, but each details his policy in his catalog.

Autograph material can also be purchased from auction firms, although there are only a limited number of these. If you have an opportunity, be sure to attend an auction sale. They're exciting fun, even if you don't join in the bidding. And each one has educational value, too, imparting useful information about autograph material and prices.

Charles Hamilton Autographs, Inc. (25 East 53rd Street, New York, New York 10022), the only firm of its type in the autograph field, schedules several auction sales in New York City each year. An elaborate catalog is prepared in advance of

If you had such Rights before it was un-
necessary. If not, you could not give your-
selves a Right you had not, without our Consent

It cannot
abrogate them

of the Legiſlative Right of this Kingdom,
whilſt the enacting part of it does no more
than abrogate the Reſolutions of the Houſe
of Repreſentatives in the North American
Colonies, which have not in themſelves the
leaſt colour of authority; and declares, that
which is apparently and certainly criminal, *neith*
only null and void.

I beg your Ldp Par-
don. They are only
Declaratory of their
own Opinion of their own Rights, & are certainly authentic;
they may indeed
like this Act be
null & void or
as yr Ldp call it
nugatory. —but
I should think
by no means
criminal.

SECONDLY,

Becauſe the particular Objections, which
have been made to the Stamp Act in North
America, and which have been adopted in
the courſe of the Debates upon this Bill for
repealing it, are in fact contradicted by un-
deniable Evidence upon our Table; it having been urged, Firſt, That all the money
to be collected by this Tax was to be annually remitted hither, and that the North A-
merican Colonies would thereby be drained
of all their ſpecie; and Secondly, That the
inſtitution of Vice Admiralty Courts in thoſe
Colonies, for the recovery of Penalties upon
Revenue Laws without Juries, is a novel
practice, by means of which his Majeſty's
Subjects in thoſe dominions, " would be de-
" prived of one of their moſt valuable Li-
" berties, Trials by Juries, and in this reſ-
" pect diſtinguiſhed from their Fellow Sub-
" jects in Great Britain;" and would like-
wiſe be liable to the greateſt Inconvenience,
Vexation

Talk with Boston
on this Head. —
Query, Court of
Common Law?

Particular Colonies drained, all Drained, —as is would
all come home. — Thoſe that would pay most of the
Tax would have least of it spent at home; it must
go to the conquered Colonies — The View of Maps
Deceives.

Benjamin Franklin's copy of the Stamp Act, a very rare piece of auto-
graph material, was offered at auction late in 1970.

each sale. Even if you are unable to attend a sale, it's wise to obtain these catalogs. Each contains a rich store of information. Write to the Hamilton firm and request information as to their availability. Each catalog costs about $2.00.

Parke-Bernet Galleries, Inc. (980 Madison Avenue, New York, New York 10021), an internationally known auction firm, well known for its sales of paintings, furniture, jewelry, and other items, conducts sales of autograph material several times a year. Parke-Bernet also publishes carefully prepared catalogs. Write for information as to their availability and cost. A handful of smaller auction firms also deal in autograph material from time to time.

Sometimes auction firms offer documents of extraordinary importance. In April of 1969, Parke-Bernet offered a copy of the first printing of the Constitution of the United States. It brought $155,000, thus establishing an auction record for an American document. A few weeks later in Philadelphia, a copy of the first printing of the Declaration of Independence, one of only sixteen known copies, was sold for the staggering sum of $404,000 to a private collector from Texas.

That summer, a Goshen, New York, woman heard about the Philadelphia sale. She had had a framed copy of the Declaration on her wall for many years and she knew it had been passed down from generation to generation. She brought the document to Parke-Bernet for an estimate of value and was told it had been printed at the same time as the copy of the Declaration sold at Philadelphia. She consigned her copy for sale; it brought $130,000 in October, 1970.

At the same sale, one of the eight known printed copies of the first draft of the Constitution of the United States, and Benjamin Franklin's copy of the Stamp Act, with notes in Franklin's hand on every page, were also offered. The former brought $80,000; the latter, $20,000.

It must be said that these sales were very special. The usual

Bidding for autograph material at the Parke-Bernet Galleries in New York City.

material offered at an auction is of a much more modest nature.

In the days before the sale takes place, the material to be offered can be examined at the auction firm. Sales representatives are on hand to answer questions or give estimates of anticipated prices, if these are not listed in the catalog. The estimates are simply meant to guide the bidder, and the final bid may be more or less than the quoted figure.

The opening pages of the catalog outline the terms of sale. If you plan to bid, or to have someone bid for you, study these pages carefully. An important point to consider is whether the material being offered is guaranteed to be genuine. Sometimes it is, while at other times material is offered "as is" or "at the buyer's risk." In such a case, it is wise to have a dealer bid for you. He will stand behind any material purchased on your behalf. His charge is 10 to 15 per cent of the bid price.

The bidding starts when the auctioneer announces the opening bid and someone meets it. While some dealers and collectors use cryptic methods for signaling their bids, the standard method is simply to raise your hand or your catalog. Parke-Bernet Galleries gives this advice to new bidders:

"Take a seat; make yourself comfortable. Follow the auctioneer's lead on limits of advance. Raise your hand in a definite signal when you wish to enter a bid, directing the signal either to the auctioneer on the rostrum or to one of the attendants in the salesroom. It's his job to relay bids to the rostrum."

If you cannot attend an auction in person, you can bid by

mail. Most catalogs contain a form on which one can enter mail bids.

When your bid is received at the auction firm, it is entered in the order book. Suppose you bid fifty dollars for an item. The bidding in the auction room—let's further suppose—opens at twenty-five dollars, then goes to thirty dollars, and then to thirty-five. If there is no additional bidding from the floor, the assistant with the order book enters your bid. "Forty dollars!" he declares. (The progression of raises, set by the auctioneer, is five dollars, so the assistant at the order book limits his raise to that amount, even though you have authorized him to bid as high as fifty dollars.)

If no one tops the forty-dollar bid, the auctioneer announces, "Sold to order!" The item is yours.

In the event that the floor bidding reached fifty dollars, the assistant at the order book would announce, "Tie with the book!" The auctioneer would then ask the floor bidders to go to fifty-five dollars. If no one did, the item would be yours, since a mail bid always has priority over a floor bid in the event of a tie.

A few days after the sale has been completed, the auction firm makes available a list of prices realized for each item. Such lists usually cost one dollar. They are valuable to have. Be aware, however, that the prices noted in such lists are not always a clear-cut indication of market prices in general. Emotion is often very much a factor in auction buying. In the fury of bidding, prices sometimes soar to extremely high levels, beyond the true value of the items. And occasionally premium material will be sold at a surprisingly low figure.

If you are interested in learning the prices auction firms have been receiving for autograph material, consult a reference book entitled *American Book-Prices Current*. Ask for it at your local library.

Auction buying can only be supplementary to the purchases you make from dealers. For one thing, an auctioned item may be bid up to a high level, well beyond your budget. Or items you are looking for may never be offered by the auction firm. With a dealer, you always pay an established price, and you can search through countless catalogs and send out innumerable want lists in an effort to obtain a desired item.

Occasionally book dealers buy or sell autographs. Naturally, they are not always as well informed about autographs as those dealers who specialize in the field exclusively, and not all book dealers guarantee their material to be genuine.

The more reputable booksellers, and a handful of noted autograph dealers as well, belong to the Antiquarian Booksellers Association of America. You may write to the organization (630 Fifth Avenue, New York, New York 10020) and request a membership list. It is free.

You may see elaborately framed autographs on sale at a local department store, often in the book department. The store will purchase a signature of, say, Dwight D. Eisenhower, then carefully enclose the signature along with a handsome photograph of Eisenhower, and perhaps other illustrative material, in a rich wooden frame behind special glareproof glass. Autographs showcased in this manner are often overpriced.

"You're not really buying an autograph when you deal with some department stores," one dealer points out. "You're buying an ornament for your home, a piece of furniture." No *real* collector would buy autographs in this manner. If you want a framed signature, it is better to buy the signature from a dealer and have it framed yourself.

Where do dealers obtain the autograph material they sell? They have three principal sources of supply: other dealers, auction sales, and private sources.

Autograph dealers study each other's catalogs to learn what material is available, and dealers in the United States maintain contact with those in foreign countries. An American dealer, for instance, might have a client who specializes in Winston Churchill material. Naturally, dealers in London would have

A form like this one enables you to bid by mail.

CHARLES HAMILTON GALLERIES, INC.
25 East 53rd Street
New York, N. Y. 10022

Please buy for me at your sale on April 23, 1970, the lots below. The amounts listed are my limit on each lot and I understand that you will purchase for me as much below this price as possible. I have read the terms of sale carefully and agree to abide by them.

References: Very truly yours,

....

....

....

Lot	Bid	Lot	Bid	Lot	Bid

LIST OF PRICES REALIZED—$1.00

greater access to Churchill material than American dealers. So the American dealer will tell his colleagues in London to inform him when Churchill documents are placed on the market. In addition, London, Paris, and Vienna have numerous autograph dealers.

Auction markets in autograph material flourish in London, Paris, and Marburg, Germany. Dealers from every part of the world attend these sales, which are held two or three times a year.

The term "private sources" usually refers to individuals who have made autographs "finds," perhaps discovering some valuable material in a musty trunk that has been stored in the attic for years. Often this material is American—letters, documents, books, maps, and other items relating to America and its history.

After two or three years, you may lose interest in collecting a particular specialty and wish to sell the autographs you've accumulated. Unless you know a private source, you will have to sell your collection to a dealer or turn it over to an auction firm. In either case, you might not receive the amount you originally paid for the material.

The dealer, when buying from a collector, has to consider his markup, the amount to be added to the cost (what he's going to pay you) to cover his expenses and assure him a profit. In other words, the price he pays for material has to be considerably less than the prevailing market price.

The auction house will charge you a fee to handle your collection. It can be as much as 20 to 30 per cent of the selling price.

Whether you sell to a dealer or allow an auction firm to sell your material for you, many factors will influence the price you receive. You may get less than you anticipate because of changing tastes. Reputations come and go. Authors, artists, and political figures in the news today may be virtual "unknowns" in five to ten years.

General economic conditions affect prices, too. You cannot expect to obtain a high price for your holdings when business, employment, and stock market values are at low levels.

Sometimes the value of collected material can increase dramatically. There are cases of collectors who have doubled or trebled their money in just two or three years, but this is an exception. Your chances of profit are best if you buy only quality material and hold it for a considerable period of time.

"Buy the best," says Charles Hamilton, "and you can never go wrong." The "best," as Mr. Hamilton defines it, is that which is "rare and fine and important." This doesn't mean you necessarily have to spend great sums of money. Buy what is considered to be premium material—important and interesting letters and documents, not cut signatures, scraps, or items in poor condition.

As a general rule, the longer you wait, the greater your chance of earning a profit. Price is based on the law of supply and demand. Demand, in the case of autographs, is ever increasing because the number of collectors is steadily rising. The supply, in many cases, is fixed. There will never be another Poe manuscript or Lincoln letter.

Besides, the amount of available historical material is constantly dwindling. Private collectors often will their collections to libraries, universities, and other public institutions. Material in such repositories is considered to be "off the market." It does not influence prices.

What all of this means is that more and more people are competing for less and less material. This situation cannot help but drive prices upward. But it is a slow and steady rise, sometimes involving decades, not merely years.

The pleasure you derive from collecting autographs shouldn't be based upon a desire to earn a profit. Real enjoyment and satisfaction come from the emotional and intellectual rewards you gain. Consider any financial gain a bonus.

As your collection grows, keep a detailed record of each purchase. The best method is to use 3″ x 5″ file cards. Each card should bear a complete description of the document, letter, or manuscript. It should tell how and when the item was acquired, who the dealer was, and the price paid.

An accurate and detailed inventory can be helpful in several ways. It serves as a formal list of your autograph properties, and can help bring to light any items you may have misplaced or that have been pilfered. The file also serves as a valuable source of price information. Always use it to compare prices you have paid in the past with current catalog listings.

7 Establishing Value

THE LETTERS or diaries of a Civil War foot soldier can command a far greater price than the signatures of the most noted generals of the time.

A handwritten letter from the pen of President Richard Nixon can be worth more than a comparable letter by George Washington.

You can purchase a cut signature of almost any one of the former United States presidents for under twenty-five dollars, but a document signed by little-known Button Gwinnett once brought $51,000 at an auction.

As these statements suggest, establishing values and setting prices in the autograph field is no simple matter. In other fields it is not nearly as difficult. In the case of stamps or coins, the two overriding factors are condition and supply. If you own a stamp that is in "mint" condition and in relatively short supply, you are likely to have a valuable prize. In autograph collecting, condition is important, and so is the matter of supply, but there are also many other factors to be weighed.

The question of authenticity is pre-eminent. Is the document or signature genuine? This is always the first question. If the answer is "yes," then certain other factors are to be evaluated, but if the answer is "no," no further consideration is necessary. The document is almost surely worthless.

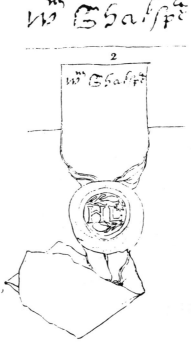

These are reproductions of existing copies of Shakespeare's signature, one of the rarest of all.

The matter of supply is always vital in establishing value. The signature of William Shakespeare is uncommonly scarce. Only six are known to exist. Each is worth a small fortune.

The names Button Gwinnett and Thomas Lynch, Jr., are well known to autograph collectors by reason of the extremely high prices their signatures bring. Both men died at relatively early ages. Both were wealthy men, without business or professional careers, which might have necessitated letter writing. Both men also happened to sign the Declaration of Independence. The army of collectors who specialize in autographs of the signers have dried up the existing supply of Gwinnett and Lynch material, and prices asked for the signatures or documents signed by either of these two are all out of proportion to their historical significance.

The importance of supply is also apparent in the case of

Charlie Chaplin's autograph is one of the few theatrical signatures with real value. (FROM THE COLLECTION OF HERMAN DARVICK)

presidential handwritten letters. After the typewriter came into common use in the early 1900's, fewer and fewer letters were written in the hand of the signer. The modern presidents, beginning with Woodrow Wilson, all signed typed correspondence, and handwritten presidential letters became extremely rare. It is a fact that a handwritten letter by Hoover or Eisenhower can be worth almost as much as one by George Washington.

When material exists in abundant supply, the opposite is true, of course. Take the case of poet Henry Wadsworth Longfellow. Longfellow would give his signature to anyone who requested it, and is said to have sent out as many as seventy autographs a day. Because his autograph is so plentiful, no great value attaches to it. Similarly, the signature of Samuel F. B. Morse, James Russell Lowell, Henry Clay, Daniel Webster, and William Cullen Bryant exist in fairly large supply, and can be purchased for relatively small sums.

Theatrical autograph material, because it is so plentiful, has only trifling value. There are some exceptions, however. The autograph of Rudolph Valentino, a romantic idol of the silent screen, and Charlie Chaplin, a Valentino contemporary, have real dollar value, and Greta Garbo's signature is extremely rare. A Garbo signed photograph can sell for as much as $100.

As for contemporary show business personalities, they are in much the same classification as professional athletes as far as market values are concerned. This is how one dealer describes market conditions: "If someone came to me with a signed photograph of Elvis Presley or Ringo Starr and wanted to sell it, I wouldn't be interested. There's no demand among serious collectors for this type of item. Only if the seller had a hundred or so signed photographs of Presley or Starr would I make him an offer."

Letters bearing the signature of a person who is still living rarely command high prices. The reason is simple. The person is still signing his name; the supply is continually building.

In addition, dealers realize that upon a person's death a great flood of that person's letters is likely to come upon the market. Most people are reluctant to sell material from a noted person while the person is living, believing that to do so would earn his disapproval. Besides, most dealers are wary about assessing a person's reputation. They prefer to leave that to history.

Supply also refers to the dealer's own stock. Suppose a dealer were offered an Albert Einstein letter, and he already had several on hand and few recent queries concerning them. He would, naturally, judge that supply was outpacing demand, and the price he would offer would reflect that judgment.

The dealer would also try to make some evaluation as to future supply, and would ask himself where the greater part of any Einstein material was housed. If it were in the hands of a private collector and about to come onto the market, he would scale down the price of the letter in question. But if it happened that the bulk of Einstein's letters and documents were

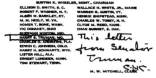

United States Senate

COMMITTEE ON INTERSTATE COMMERCE

This letter from Senator Truman. — S.H.C. —

Hot Springs, Ark
Oct 15 1943

Hon. Carl H. Claudy,
Washington, D.C.

My dear Carl:— Your good letter of Sept 30 just now caught up with me. I have been going around the country inspecting defense areas and plants. I slip in unannounced and in that way get some of the truth. Have been here for four days taking treatments at this good Gov't Hospital for my bad tooth and some sinus trouble. Will be on my way again tomorrow. The Grand Lodge improves with time. Hope to visit with you when I get back. I have a raincheck.. you know You have my best.

Sincerely, Harry.

A handwritten letter is usually more valuable than one that is merely typewritten and signed. (FROM THE COLLECTION OF HERMAN DARVICK)

tucked away in a library or other repository, it would be an entirely different matter. Only material on the open market influences price.

Everyone realizes that another primary consideration is the name and status of the writer or signer of a document. In the

United States, the greatest value is attached to autograph material of the presidents, the signers of the Declaration of Independence, and well-known world leaders, statesmen, generals, authors, composers, and scientists.

Condition is of paramount importance, too. Mildewing or fading, tears, cuts, or stains—any of these diminish value. Ink is preferred to pencil. The latter smudges and fades.

Just as important as the name of the signer, and sometimes a greater factor than condition, is the matter of contents, or what the document says.

At a recent auction, a letter of Major General George Mercer Brooke, a page and a half in length, written at Pensacola, Florida, on June 1, 1818, brought $285. Brooke is not a noted figure in American history, so the high price surprised many— but not anyone who took the time to read the letter carefully.

Spain officially yielded Florida to the United States in 1819, and the letter gave significant background information about the ceding. "After a most tedious . . . march of twenty days through wilderness," the letter said, "we arrived at this place, which we enter'd without resistance, notwithstanding the repeated declarations of the Spanish officers that we should be fired on." The letter continued with a description of the Battle of Pensacola: "A severe canonading commenc'd at sunrise, lasted that Day and part of the next, when he thought proper to capitulate. A Flag of Truce was rec'd just as the storming parties had been formed."

The catalog described the letter as having "superb contents." Indeed, it was true.

Never fail to consider contents. President Nixon's signature on a letter to a supporter, expressing gratitude for his backing on a particular issue, is valuable, of course, but Nixon's signature on a directive that establishes government or perhaps military policy—a document important in United States history— is of infinitely more value. A letter in which Alexander Calder

September 25, 1935

Mr. William H. Sealy
Kosse, Texas

Dear Mr. Sealy:

This is in reply to your letter of September 23.

I am enclosing herewith a bulletin which explains the type of aid available to college students under the National Youth Administration, as well as the requirements and procedure necessary to securing it.

Students who have been awarded high school scholarships are eligible to participate.

As you will notice in the attached outline, the National Youth Administration pays wages, averaging $15.00 a month, in return for part-time work done in connection with schools. This work is of a socially desirable character, and is arranged so that it will not interfere with the students' scholastic duties.

In making application for one of these NYA part-time jobs, the student must write direct to the president of the college, he or she, wishes to attend.

This program is now under way in Texas, and colleges have been accepting applications for some time. It is possible that plans had not been fully developed at the time the college president told you that no such funds were available.

Denominational and religious colleges are eligible to participate in the National Youth Administration program.

If I can furnish you with any further information concerning the NYA, I shall be happy to do so.

With all good wishes, I am

Sincerely yours,

Lyndon B. Johnson
NYA Director for Texas

LBJ CHA
encl.

This is an interesting presidential item, but a Lyndon Johnson letter is likely to be of greater value if signed by him during 1963-1968, the years of his presidency. (FROM THE COLLECTION OF PAUL HARTUNIAN)

discusses the basic principles of the mobile has infinitely more value than one written in his youth, before he achieved international renown.

Also on the subject of letters, the matter of association is important. To whom was the letter written? A letter from Thomas Jefferson to Alexander Hamilton is likely to be more highly prized than one Jefferson wrote to any minor political figure.

102

The same holds true today. A letter from poet Wallace Stevens to another contemporary literary figure is more desirable than a letter from Stevens to, say, a real estate dealer.

When the letter was written—the date—must also be considered. The matter of date refers not so much to the relative newness or oldness of the material, but more as to how the date relates to the signer. A letter written by a Civil War general and dated 1877 would not be likely to be as valuable as a similar letter written between 1861 and 1865, the years spanned by the war. The letter of a signer of the Declaration of Independence and dated 1776, the year the Declaration itself was signed, is sure to be priced at several times the price of a letter dated 1775 or 1777, as long as they are about the same in content. Letters by authors or scientists, composers, or engineers are usually more valued when written during peak periods of their careers than those written during their years of retirement.

Fadism affects values, too. A person wins sudden acclaim or experiences a spurt in popularity, and the value of his signature on any meaningful document skyrockets. Don't be trapped into buying material that is high priced simply because of the public's whim.

More than one dealer believes that autograph material of many contemporary American artists and some writers is currently being sold at inflated prices. "A great many people who are popular today are almost certain to be forgotten in the years to come," says one dealer. "There is no real value to their work. They are terribly temporary."

Private and public libraries are certain to offer valuable research material concerning your specialty.

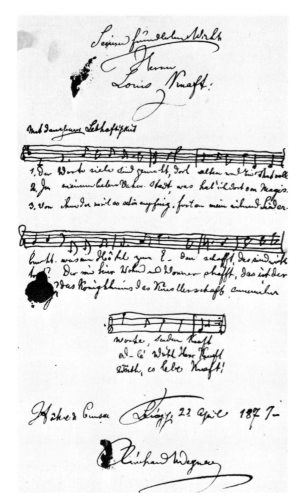

This document has important value for several reasons. First, the name of the signer, Richard Wagner, the great German composer; second, its contents, original verses and bars of music; third, the fact that it was written in Wagner's own hand. (FROM THE COLLECTION OF ELMER J. JEROME)

Serious collectors keep price lists referring to their specialty. If they are collecting documents and manuscripts of George Bernard Shaw, for instance, they maintain a careful record of all dealers' listings of Shaw material—the dealer's name, the date, a description of the item offered, and the price. Information of this type, collected over a long period, helps one to spot bargain-priced items.

It requires long experience and substantial knowledge to be able to appraise accurately autograph material. How could a dealer put a price on a Civil War letter referring to the Battle of Antietam without knowing the significance of the engagement?

How could he tell you the value of a manuscript in the handwriting of Edgar Lee Masters without knowing Masters' standing as a poet?

You have to become an authority in your special field. Read all you can about the personality you collect or the field. Get to know all you can about that personality or the field. Get to know other collectors who have the same specialty.

No matter what area you specialize in, there is certain to be a library or other research institution which can offer you information and assistance. Your public library has available several directories containing information about these repositories.

The very best is *The National Union Catalog of Manuscript Collections*, a reference book which has been compiled and published by the Library of Congress, and which gives the nature and location of all significant bodies of unpublished research material in the United States. It describes 18,417 different collections in 616 separate institutions. The index classifies tens of thousands of subjects by place names and personal names.

This clay Babylonian cylinder with cuneiform characters, which dates to about 2100 B.C., is part of the manuscript collection of the New York Public Library.

Dear Sir,   *New York april 6. 1789*

On the Sunday sennight after leaving Mount Vernon I arrived here, where to my surprise I found that a quorum of the Senate was not assembled, and but a small majority of Representatives. On this day we went to business, and to my very great satisfaction I heard an unanimous vote of the electing States in favor of calling you to the honorable office of President of the United States. Before this period, I judged it might not be acceptable to speak my sentiments to you on this subject; but now, I hope I may be permitted to express my ardent hope that your inclinations may correspond with the united wish of America, that you should preside over those Councils which you have so greatly contributed to render independent. Indeed, I am sure that the public happiness, which I know you have so much at heart, will be very insecure without your acceptance.

The two Houses feel the necessity of proceeding to the preparation of some important business, that it may be in all possible forwardness against your arrival. That

---

334

that of securing the Impost on the Spring arrivals seems to be the most pressing.

An Express goes also to Mr. Adams immediately to inform him of his election to the Office of Vice President. I pray to be remembered affectionately to your Lady and the family at Mount Vernon.

With every sentiment of respect and esteem I have the honor to be dear Sir your most affectionate and obedient servant

Richard Henry Lee

Its incredible contents make this letter a priceless treasure. Richard Henry Lee, a delegate to the Continental Congress from Virginia, is the signer. The letter was addressed to George Washington, and in it Lee informs Washington that he has been unanimously elected president and urges him to accept the office. (FROM THE COLLECTION OF NATHANIEL E. STEIN)

The largest and most notable of all autograph and manuscript collections is to be found in the Library of Congress in Washington, D. C. It is made up of more than three thousand separate collections totaling approximately thirty million manuscripts. A staff of 3,500 is required to maintain the enormous array of material. This great treasure house includes the personal papers of most American presidents, as well as those of other statesmen, military leaders, scientists, and other individuals prominent in American history.

While the largest and most stunning collection of material is maintained by the federal government, private institutions play an extremely active role in bringing together and preserving valuable letters, diaries, manuscripts, and documents. Historical societies are one example. Most states have at least one historical society actively engaged in collecting manuscripts, and there are city and county historical societies as well.

Experts have called this document—of immense value because of the signatures it bears—one of the key documents in American history. After the signing of the Declaration of Independence, Benjamin Owen Tyler was assigned to make facsimile copies of the document for the signers and others. Below is a page from Tyler's order book for copies.
(FROM THE COLLECTION OF NATHANIEL E. STEIN)

The Directory of Historical Societies and Agencies in the United States and Canada, compiled by the American Association for State and Local History, offers information on 3,565 societies and agencies. It gives the name and address of each, its membership, and indicates the library and museum facilities offered. Your public library is likely to have a copy of this reference book.

The Directory of Special Libraries and Information Centers may also be helpful. This source gives information on research collections maintained by colleges and universities, government agencies, and nonprofit organizations.

University libraries represent another important storehouse of historical material. Some of their collections are of enormous size. The University of Texas library in Austin has in store close to four million documents, with particular emphasis on the history of the American South, American poetry, English literature, and Mexican history.

Duke University in Durham, North Carolina, has almost three million manuscripts dealing principally with eighteenth- and nineteenth-century English literature, the American South, and Italian history. Yale University is world renown for its collection of James Boswell-Samuel Johnson material.

Private collectors in the United States have made a significant contribution to the preservation of manuscripts and documents concerning the nation's history. Much of the material now housed in university libraries originally belonged to private collectors who bequeathed their collections to the institutions.

American financier J. Pierpont Morgan was one of the most noted of all collectors of manuscript material. He began by collecting autographs of United States presidents and went on to build a priceless collection of documents and letters, and medieval and Renaissance illuminated manuscripts. Today, the collection is maintained at the Morgan Library in New York City, where portions of it are always on display.

8 Presidential Autographs

IT IS A HANDWRITTEN letter about the size of this page, slightly worn, and a bit yellowed. A small tear appears in one margin and it bears two tiny holes that look like pin pricks. "Executive Mansion," says the letterhead.

The letter is addressed to Civil War General Meade at Warrenton, Virginia, and is dated September 18, 1863. It reads:

> Is Albert Jones, of Co. K 3rd Maryland volunteers, to be shot on Friday next? If so, please state to me the general features of the case.

The letter is signed "A. Lincoln."

Historians have established that Albert Jones was "killed" on September 18. Why? Did the letter go undelivered? Did President Lincoln have a change of heart and decide not to interfere in the matter? Or was the message indeed delivered, but ignored by General Meade?

These are some of the questions the letter poses. But the letter is much more than an intriguing historical footnote. On more than one occasion President Lincoln was moved to intercede on behalf of soldiers awaiting the death sentence. This letter, in his own hand, is fascinating proof of his compassion.

The letter is also an exemplification of the field of presidential autographs, the most popular single field in autograph collecting. It is not difficult to understand why, for presidential documents often give a rare insight into the character and temperament of the men who shaped the course of United States history.

Documents signed by each of the presidents are readily available, although in the case of the early presidents, prices are quite high. There are not only letters available, but signed items of every type—military commissions, land grants, and ships' papers. There are inscribed books, autographed photographs and portraits, signed checks, souvenir White House cards, and even lottery tickets.

One of the most unusual of presidential items was offered at an auction sale at Parke-Bernet Galleries in New York City late in 1970. It consisted of a long and detailed list of "sundry items" entirely in the hand of George Washington, which were "to be sent by Robt. Cary Esq. & Compa. of London" for use at Mount Vernon. Written when Washington was twenty-eight and in the second year of his marriage, the document imparts a clear understanding of the man's preciseness, his careful attention to minute details.

A handwritten Lincoln or Washington letter is beyond the means of most collectors (Washington's list of sundries sold for $6,500), but there is a great array of material that is available from dealers at prices that are modest. Many, many collectors specialize in presidential signatures, often referred to as "cut"

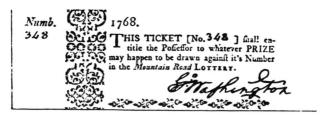

George Washington's signature sometimes is found on lottery tickets of his day.

110

Invoice of Sundry Goods to be sent by Robt Cary Esqr & Compa
for the use of George Washington. — Virginia

1 pair Crimson Velvet Breeches
1 pair black knit Silk Ditto
1 do black — Ditto worsted ditto
1 do fine light col. Silk Shag ditto
2 pieces Irish Holland — a 6/.-
1 piece Cambrick for Ruffles — or
    something else proper, if Cambrick
    is not to be had. —
1 piece Irish Linnen — a 2/.-
4 yards fine book Muslin — a 10/.
2 ditto fine white Gauze —
1 piece fine Canting
1 piece of white Callico — a 40/.-
1 piece of bird eye Diaper for Towels
2 pieces best Nankeen with buttons
    & Mohair to suit Ditto
1 White Persian quilted Petticoat
2 Satten Bonnets. —
2 pair dble Channel Pumps
4 do strong Shoes.
2 do very neat Stichd & bound Pumps
12 Rolls best Shoe blacking. —
1 pair Womans black Satten Shoes
1 pair ditto — white Ditto
2 pair neat black everlasting Ditto
    all made accord g to y measure sent —
2 pair Woman s black everlasting Ditto d
2 do strong leath r Ditto of large Sizes
6 pair Mens neat white Gloves —
2 pair ditto of Norway Doe — above y
    middle Size — Stichd Tops -
6 pr Womans white kid Gloves
6 do ditto Mitts —
2 pr colourd Gloves
4 do ditto Mitts
1 Groce Shirt Buttons —

4 pair Tabby Stays according to y measure
6 Knots & Breast Knots -
3 Egrets
2 Fashionable Fans —
4 pieces fine Diaper Tape
6 M. Minikin Pins
6 M. Short whites
6 M. large Ditto
1 Comb Case, Combs & Powder Box
6 fine horn Combs & Comb brushes
2 Bottles Waskerns low dried Scotch Snuff
1 dble bitted bridle with 2 p Reins
4 Sirsingles —
6 Girths
3 Sadle Cloths
6 strong snaffle bridles
2 doz n Hempen halters with flat heads
6 Coach Whip Thongs. —
2 Chair Whip Ditto
1 Doz n horse Collars. —
1 Set of Strong Waggon Harness for
    5 Middle sizd Horses. — NB they
    may be strong, but not heavy. —
1 doz n beer & Cyder Glasses
1½ doz n Punch ditto
2 doz n wine Glasses all of y newest Fash
½ doz n Milk Pots Glass
6 China Mugs two of a sort. —
6 Ditto Potting Pots 2 of a size — none large
2 large Stone Churns, each to hold 10 Gall t
6 doz n earthen Milk Pans —
1 doz n strong Mugs different sizes
½ doz n ditto Piggins — 2 of them to hold
    a Gall each — 2 a Bottle each & 2 a Quart
1 doz n Stone Chamber Pots
1 doz n Ditto Wash Basons

A list of "sundry goods" for use at Mount Vernon prepared by George
Washington.

signatures, since they have been snipped from a document or letter. In days past, it was widely held that the individual's signature was what was valuable, while the document to which it was affixed was thought to be meaningless.

A good amount of Washington material has been subjected to the cruelty of clipping. One example is well known. Before he left the White House, Washington drafted a farewell address which he later discarded in favor of a second version, a version which included material provided by Alexander Hamilton and James Madison.

The early draft was obtained by Jared Sparks, an early president of Harvard University and a biographer of Washington. Historians and other interested parties often wrote to Sparks to ask for samples of Washington's handwriting. To fulfill the requests, Sparks would simply snip a section from the farewell address manuscript.

He never bothered to make a copy of the speech in its entirety. Through the years, fragments of the manuscript have continued to appear from time to time, but scholars have never been able to piece together the whole thing. What did Washington mean to say before Hamilton and Madison presented him with their thoughts? No one may ever know. It is an historical puzzle with some of the pieces missing.

Washington's is the scarcest of all clipped signatures, selling for about $200. Lincoln's is almost as rare, and a Jefferson signature sells for approximately $100. Most others are not expensive. The signature of Herbert Hoover, Rutherford B. Hayes, Dwight Eisenhower, and Harry Truman can be purchased for ten dollars or less.

No person signs his name in exactly the same way twice, so there are price variations among the signatures of the presidents. The boldness of the signature, the quality of the paper, the type of ink—all of these affect value. Sometimes the chief executive signs his name in full, while at other times he may use only his

George Washington

Franklin D. Roosevelt

James Monroe

Harry S. Truman

Abraham Lincoln

John F. Kennedy

Theodore Roosevelt

In signing letters and other documents, United States presidents sometimes resort to mere initials.

initials. Naturally, the latter has less appeal than the former.

Up until the administration of Ulysses S. Grant, it was customary for the chief executive to write out his signature on any slip of paper in responding to an autograph request. But Grant had small cards prepared bearing the engraved heading "Executive Mansion" and would sign his name on these. Theodore Roosevelt changed the heading on the card to read "The White House." Such cards are sought more avidly than cut signatures, so they cost more.

Recent presidents—Richard Nixon, Lyndon Johnson, and

Some collectors specialize in autograph cards signed by the presidents.

John F. Kennedy—also used signature cards to fulfill collector requests. However, the signature was a facsimile or created by an Autopen.

Some collectors specialize in checks signed by presidents. Dealers' catalogs often list these. Recent listings offered checks by Theodore Roosevelt or James Garfield for seventy-five dollars.

If you have ever received a letter from a federal official, you have probably noticed the printed frank in the upper right-hand corner of the envelope where the stamp would ordinarily be. In days past, it was usual for the person granted the franking privilege to personally sign the envelope, and many collectors specialize in hand-signed franks of the presidents. An envelope personally free-franked by James Buchanan recently sold for thirty-five dollars. An envelope bearing James Monroe's signature went for $100.

Of course, hand-signed franks are exceptionally rare today. An envelope addressed and franked by John Kennedy while a senator, and postmarked Palm Beach, Florida, December 17, 1955, was recently listed in a dealer's catalog at $1,500.

Congress also gives the franking privilege to widows of presidents. Among those who have exercised the privilege are Lucretia R. Garfield, Frances F. Cleveland, Mary Lord Harrison, Edith K. Roosevelt, Edith Bolling Wilson, Grace Coolidge, and Jacqueline Kennedy.

There are many people who specialize in collecting material bearing the signatures of members of the families of the presidents. More than a few collectors specialize in items signed by First Ladies. Martha Washington's signature, perhaps the most sought, is worth approximately $150. Dolley Madison used to write out and sign religious poems for those who requested them, and dealers sometimes have these available. One costs about fifty dollars. The signatures of Eliza Monroe, Hannah Van Buren, Rachel Jackson, and Sarah Polk are extremely rare.

Items signed by the sons, daughters, mothers, fathers, sisters, brothers, and even cousins of the presidents are sought, too. A brief letter of Julie Nixon and an inscribed photograph of John Eisenhower were recently listed in a dealer's catalog for $7.50 each.

Some presidential material is available by writing for it. Of course, the president himself is not going to answer personally a letter from an ordinary citizen, but the wife of the president may. Mrs. Nixon has always been scrupulous about her correspondence. Unlike other White House occupants of recent times, she shunned the use of the Autopen and facsimile or proxy signatures. Any letter that bears Mrs. Nixon's signature was also probably signed by her. She is said to have autographed fifty to one hundred photographs each week in answer to mail requests.

Checks signed by the presidents are another specialty. (FROM THE COLLECTION OF HERMAN DARVICK)

Mrs. Nixon has a full realization of how much letters from the presidential family mean to the recipients. "They're shown to neighbors," she once said, "and eventually appear in the paper, and they're very important to the people who receive them."

When writing, don't overlook retired presidents. Harry Truman was often cooperative about answering autograph requests after he left the White House, and pithy letters from him concerning politics, government, history, and some personalities are not exactly rare.

Herbert Hoover was very fond of writing letters, and he once estimated that he wrote approximately ten thousand letters a year. Almost any courteous letter to the thirty-first president brought a reply. He continued to answer letters faithfully after his term of office ended. Often the letters Hoover received were from schoolchildren, and he replied to these with warmth and sometimes humor.

One letter Hoover received was as follows:

Dear President Hoover,
    I am almost nine. I am in 3rd grade—Elementary school. I am in the first reading group.
    I like History. Did you like being President? How are You?
    Please wright. I now you are busy.

This was Hoover's reply:

My dear Joe:
    I am glad you like history.
    As to your question, being President in time of unemployment and hardship is not too happy an experience.

Another letter Hoover received said:

Dear Mr. Hoover,
    We are starting a collection of autographs. If you could possibly spare the time, would you please send us your real signature? We would prefer this to a photostatic copy.
    Our collection of autographs is just a hobby.

To this Hoover answered:

My dear Bonnie:

I can understand your preference for genuine autographs rather than photostats. This is genuine.

I was delighted to see that you are not a professional autograph hunter. Once upon a time one of those asked me for three autographs. I inquired why. He said, "It's takes two of yours to get one of Babe Ruth's."

If you plan to buy presidential material from dealers, keep in mind the points covered about value and prices. The signature itself—that is, who signed the document—is extremely important, but it alone does not establish the value of an item. What is signed and the contents of the document are just as important.

Take material signed by George Washington, for example. A Washington pen-and-ink signature, cut from a letter or other document, is worth about $200.

A step up the value ladder come military discharges. During his tenure as president and commander in chief of the military, Washington signed the discharge papers of every soldier who served honorably in the American Revolution. So while such a document is valuable—the going price was about $400 in 1970 —it is not as rare as some other types of Washington material.

In scanning a dealer's catalog, you might come upon an entry describing a Washington letter, however brief, that outlines government policy or recommends certain battle plans before a new historic military engagement. A document of this type would be worth approximately $1,000 to $5,000.

There are Washington letters of even greater rarity, ones in which the first president expresses his discouragement over the failure of his ideas or lack of progress in his plans, or in which he speaks in glowing terms about one of his friends. Letters of this type give us a rare glimpse of what Washington was really like. A letter of this type can command a price approaching $20,000.

Items signed by the wives of the presidents and First Ladies are collected, too. (FROM THE COLLECTION OF HERMAN DARVICK)

The matter of when the document was signed influences value. Some collectors limit their efforts to material dated with the actual term of office of the signer, and as a result, material of this nature is more difficult to obtain and higher priced. For instance, letters or other documents signed by Lyndon Johnson as senator and vice-president can be purchased for less than fifty dollars, but material bearing Johnson's signature as president sometimes sells for five times that amount.

In the case of modern presidents, dealers often offer signed letters, while documents are seldom seen. But in the case of the first presidents, the reverse is true: letters are relatively scarce, while documents are much more common.

The land grant was one such document. In the country's early days, tracts of land, up to fifteen thousand acres in size, were given to veterans of the Revolutionary War, to citizens in compensation for losses suffered during the Revolution, and to individuals who had purchased land at auction. Tens of thousands of grants were issued, and each had to be signed personally by the president. Not until 1833, during the administration of Andrew Jackson, did Congress authorize a clerk or secretary to

118

sign on the president's behalf. The most coveted grants are those signed by Washington and Jefferson.

The early presidents were also required to sign "sea letters," special documents permitting United States ships to leave American ports and requesting courtesy from foreign officials. Many

The Mount Vernon Ladies Association gathered together this collection of Washington family autographs.

such documents were issued for whaling ships, and they bear the name of the vessel and the declaration "found for Atlantic Ocean whaling."

Early presidents also personally signed military commissions and civil appointments. Many of the former were decorated with brightly colored flags, and, depending upon the branch of the service, ocean waves or cannon balls. A commission makes a striking addition to any collection.

Up until Andrew Jackson's tenure, presidents were also required to sign government patents. These documents also bore the signature of the secretary of state, and attached to each was a detailed description of the invention. Presidentially signed patents are avidly sought.

All presidents, right up until the present day, have signed proclamations. Each one is exceedingly valuable. The most famous of all bears Lincoln's signature. It is the Emancipation Proclamation.

The listings that follow were culled from the catalogs of several dealers, and are representative of the offerings of modestly priced presidential material as of late 1970:

CLEVELAND, GROVER. A.L.S., 2 full pp, 8vo, State of New York, Executive Chamber, Albany, 1883. To Mrs. Frank H. Martin expressing appreciation for the naming of a son after him. Fold damage mended $12.00

CLEVELAND, GROVER. D.S., 4pp, fol., Buffalo, N. Y., February 8, 1862 . . . . $35.00
Interesting Erie Canal boat mortgage issued on the "Lake Erie of Buffalo." The last seven lines of page 3 and all of page 4 are in the hand of Cleveland, so this could be said to include an A.D.S. of the 24-year-old future President. Cleveland has signed as the Commissioner of Deeds of the City of Buffalo. Bearing two desirable U.S. revenue stamps.

COOLIDGE, CALVIN. Autograph signature on White House card.
$12.00

February 25 1884

My dear Sir

It gives me pleasure to comply with your request.

Very faithfully yours

Chester A. Arthur

EISENHOWER, DWIGHT. Autograph signature on the cover of the April 11, 1964, issue of the Saturday Evening Post containing his article, "Why I Am A Republican." $30.00

GARFIELD, JAMES A. Autograph signature—"J. A. Garfield M.C." —on address portion of envelope postmarked "Washington, D.C. Free Mar. 1". $22.50

GARFIELD, JAMES A. D.S. Washington, 1875. Check drawn on the Sergeant-at-Arms, U. S. House of Representatives, payable to "Myself Cash," and signed $47.50

GRANT, ULYSSES S. A.L.S. 1p, 4to. "Head Quarters, Dist. of West Ten. Memphis, July 3, 1862." $75.00
To Col. D. C. Anthony, Provost Marshal, ordering the release of S. A. Meacham on parole.

GRANT, ULYSSES S. Autograph signature on a card . . . $10.00

GRANT, ULYSSES S. D.S. 1p, 4to. Washington, May 31, 1876. Order to affix the seal on a pardon. $60.00

HARRISON, BENJAMIN. Autograph signature on verso of visiting card. With original envelope $25.00

HAYES, RUTHERFORD B. A.L.S. 1p, 8vo. Executive Department, State of Ohio, Columbus, 1876. Name of the recipient has been deleted. "You are strongly commended for Police Commissioner," etc. $50.00

HOOVER, HERBERT. L.S. 1p, 4to. New York, January 26, 1942. Appreciative regrets that he cannot accept an invitation as he will be on Pacific Coast $20.00

JOHNSON, ANDREW. Autograph signature on card dated by him, March 27, 1869 . . . . $35.00

JOHNSON, ANDREW. D.S. 1pp, fol. Washington, March 5, 1867. Bears stamped signatures of both President Johnson and Edwin M. Stanton, Secretary of War, registered in ink by General E. D. Townsend $25.00
Very handsome ornate vellum document appointing Robert E. Clary as the Assistant Quartermaster General. Since Johnson injured his right hand shortly after taking office, nearly ninety per cent of the official papers requiring his signature bear his printed signature. Johnson was impeached because he removed Stanton from Office, being charged with violating the Tenure of Office Act passed by Congress over Johnson's veto on March 2, 1867, just three days before this document was issued.

McKINLEY, WILLIAM. D.S. 2pp, 4to. Ohio, November 18, 1870.
$25.00
Indictment for assault and battery with intent to murder. Signed by McKinley as Prosecuting Attorney for Stark County, Ohio.

ROOSEVELT, FRANKLIN. L.S. 1p, 4to. Warm Springs, Georgia, April 9, 1928 . . . . $30.00

ROOSEVELT, THEODORE. D.S. New York City, 1911. Check drawn on the Astor Trust Company for $352.70 payable to James L. Clark $35.00

TRUMAN, HARRY S LS. 1p, 4to. Independence, Mo., May 12, 1964. Truman expresses his regrets he cannot speak at the press club at the University of Wisconsin $15.00

TRUMAN, HARRY S L.S. 1p, 4to. Washington, D.C., 1935. Written to the Veterans Administration on behalf of a veteran. Punch holes at top; wrinkled $35.00

An unusual presidential item —an order form for a book, signed by President McKinley.

ONLY AUTHORIZED EDITION

Contract No. *1-*

_____ *1899*

THE WOOLFALL COMPANY
New York

Gentlemen:

I hereby subscribe for one copy of

> ## The Life and Letters of Admiral Dewey

complete in one Royal Imperial 8vo volume, with over two hundred and fifty illustrations, including Coats-of-Arms in color; also many portraits and maps, at $ *six dollars* *per copy, bound in* *Half-Levant*

Please deliver the same at the address and as nearly as convenient according to the directions given below.

I agree to pay the sum of $ *6.00* *on delivery of the work.* *Cash*,

Regular Subscription Prices	Special Introductory Prices
CLOTH EDITION, $4.50	CLOTH EDITION, $2.50
HALF-LEVANT " 6.00	HALF-LEVANT " 3.50
FULL " " 7.50	FULL " " 4.50

Name *William McKinley*

Business Address *Washington D.C.*

Residence *Canton Ohio.*

Deliver at _____ *When* _____

VAN BUREN, MARTIN. Partly printed D.S. 1p, fol. Albany, N. Y., August 1815. Signed twice as Attorney-General of New York $30.00
Complaint against David Philo who owes the State $32.93. Over forty words in Van Buren's hand. Slight tears in folds.

Once in a very great while, a person will come upon a presidential letter or document while rummaging about in the attic. One of the most extraordinary finds of this type occurred early in 1969, when two huge pine chests containing more than a

The Presidential Office at the Truman Library in Independence, Missouri.

thousand pieces of correspondence that once belonged to President Millard Fillmore were found in a forty-room farmhouse in New Haven in northern New York state. The discovery was front page news in every part of the country.

About seventy of the letters were from Dorothea Dix, nineteenth-century philanthropist and reformer, and an author of several books for children. The letters showed her "deep personal interest" in Fillmore, causing more than one newspaper to headline: "Love Notes Written to Millard Fillmore Found."

The material in the trunks had a fascinating history. President Fillmore willed his papers to his son. In the son's will, the papers were to be destroyed, but the executor chose to ignore the instructions and put the papers into storage. On the son's death, all of Fillmore's papers went to the Buffalo Historical

Society—except the two trunks. They were overlooked.

In the early 1900's, Charles Shepherd, a Buffalo businessman, obtained the trunks from a friend of the Fillmore family. Shepherd stored them away and forgot about them. When Shepherd died in 1968, his surviving niece bequeathed his house and its contents to the State University of New York. The next year a university professor made the discovery.

Among the letters in the collection, there were many from political figures of Fillmore's time—William H. Seward, Horace Greeley, and Franklin Pierce, Fillmore's successor as president.

Until fairly recent times, there was no standard procedure for caring for presidential papers, and many were lost, damaged, or destroyed, or, as in the case of the Fillmore letters, simply misplaced. Because of the enormous increase in the amount of papers over the past forty years, it became impossible for former presidents to store and protect them properly. The word "papers," incidentally, refers not only to autograph material and all printed items, books included, but to the countless gifts a president receives, many of which have artistic merit as well as commemorative value.

It is generally agreed that presidential papers are a national treasure, and, as such, it is vital that they be protected, preserved, and made available to scholars and students who seek a fuller understanding of the president and the period in which he worked. With these thoughts in mind, Congress passed the Presidential Libraries Act of 1955, which provided for the housing and care of the papers, books, and gifts of any president who wished to present them to the nation. The following presidential libraries have been established, most as a direct result of the Act:

Herbert Hoover Library, West Branch, Iowa
Franklin D. Roosevelt Library, Hyde Park, New York

Harry S Truman Library, Independence, Missouri
Dwight D. Eisenhower Library, Abilene, Kansas
John F. Kennedy Library, Cambridge, Massachusetts
Lyndon B. Johnson Library, Austin, Texas

Under the provisions of the Act, each of the libraries is staffed and operated by the National Archives and Records Service of the General Services Administration. Each of the libraries offers a great deal more than simply facilities for the storage, preservation, and use of papers, books, and other historical materials. The Harry S Truman Library, for example, features a museum with exhibits devoted to the nature and history of the presidency. The displayed items include the presidential seal as redesigned during the Truman administration, jeweled swords and daggers from the King and Crown Prince of Saudi Arabia, and items autographed by Winston Churchill and other world leaders. The east gallery of the museum is devoted to an exhibit concerning the battleship *Missouri* and features the original Japanese instrument of surrender signed aboard the vessel in 1945.

The autograph material on display, on loan from the National Archives, includes: Jefferson's request to Congress for funds for the Lewis and Clark Expedition; pardons issued by Lincoln during the Civil War; Truman's V-E Day proclamation, and Kennedy's Executive Order establishing the Peace Corps.

As of 1970, the Truman Library housed an estimated eight million papers, with more being donated all the time. They are stored in specially equipped steel and concrete stack areas where the temperature and humidity are carefully controlled. Photographs, sound recordings, and motion picture films are similarly protected.

If you have an opportunity, don't fail to visit a Presidential Library. It is sure to be a rewarding experience. Information about displays and facilities at any one of the libraries can be obtained by writing the National Archives and Records Section

Noted collector Nathaniel E. Stein owns this and other pages from Washington's discarded inaugural address.

(Eighth Street and Pennsylvania Avenue N.W., Washington, D. C. 20408).

Scholars and students have applauded the concept of organizing research facilities dedicated to outstanding national figures, and the idea is spreading. Thus, we now have the Rayburn Library (after former Speaker of the House of Representatives, Samuel Rayburn) at Bonham, Texas; the Douglas MacArthur Library at Norfolk, Virginia; the George C. Marshall Library (after the World War II military leader and secretary of state) on the campus of the Virginia Military Institute; and the Estes Kefauver Library (after the former senator) at the University of Tennessee.

9 Autograph Care and Display

AUTOGRAPH MATERIAL is essentially paper and ink, and since both of these are somewhat perishable, your collection requires special treatment. The more valuable the items in your collection, the greater should be your concern about how they are stored and displayed.

First, some don'ts:

Never make the slightest mark on a letter or other document. Never cut anything out of a letter. Your objective should be to store the material in precisely the same condition it arrives.

Store all material perfectly flat. Unfold letters or other items that may arrive folded. In time, a fold becomes a crease, and a crease becomes a tear.

Remove all paper clips or staples. They cause unsightly mars. Some rust and stain. Rubber bands stain, too.

Never use any foreign substance on any item of autograph material. This includes glue, paste, rubber cement—any type of adhesive. Virtually every type of adhesive deteriorates and discolors in time, causing damage.

Never use tape, transparent or otherwise, in putting material into an album. Never use plastic spray as a preservative.

The simplest and least expensive method of storing your collection is to place the items in cardboard folders, then arrange the folders in alphabetical order, or by subject, in a metal file cabinet. Letter-size file folders cost slightly more than a dollar a dozen. File pockets—folders which are closed on three sides and have the ability to expand—are suitable for the larger items.

Some collectors keep an insect repellent in the lower part of the file cabinet. Even an ordinary moth repellent, such as flaked naphthalene, will help to ward off silverfish and bookworms.

Excessive moisture stimulates fungus growth, resulting in mildew or foxing stains, either one of which is evidenced by discoloration. You can prevent damage of this type by storing material in a dry place.

Too much heat can be just as harmful as too much moisture. It causes paper fibers to become brittle and documents will deteriorate as a result. Beware of storing material in the attic or any other place that can become excessively warm.

Many collectors store and display material in three-ring binders, the type used for schoolwork. The binder should have heavy board covers and nickel-plated metals. The rings should be spaced for standard punching.

As pages, use transparent sheet protectors. These are available at your local stationery store, and are prepunched for use in three-ring binders. You simply insert the items to be displayed. Don't paste them down! After they're inserted, you can pass the album around to show your collection to your friends and there is no risk that the material will become finger-marked or otherwise soiled.

Transparent sheets are usually made of acetate, which does an adequate job, but your material will be better protected if you use Mylar sheets. Mylar, a relatively new material, is lighter in weight, gets high marks for scratch resistance and clarity, will not tear, and is unaffected by temperature, moisture, or age. A dozen 9″ x 11″ Mylar sheet protectors, which can be

Most collectors use transparent sheet protectors to store and display material.

used to store and display at least twenty-four different items, costs about three dollars.

Your local stationery shop is also likely to have available multiring presentation binders with transparent sheet protectors in sizes ranging up to 18″ x 24″. A binder of this size, with ten sheet protectors, costs about twenty-five dollars. A good many collectors prefer this size, storing several items to a page.

If you specialize in signatures on index cards or first-day covers, there are albums available that offer both visibility and protection for material of this size. Inquire at a stationery store or hobby shop.

A really important letter or document should receive special treatment. A Springfield, Massachusetts, collector recently obtained a letter signed by Dwight D. Eisenhower in 1945. Eisenhower was then Supreme Commander of the Allied Expeditionary Force in Europe. The letter was addressed to a Mrs. Helen LaMontagne and thanked her for ". . . her expression of good wishes to me and all the forces serving under my command..."

The collector used the letter as the principal display piece in a special album he prepared. It contained several transparent sheets arranged in the following sequence:

1. The title page, a capsule description of the document—Dwight D. Eisenhower (L.S.) to Helen LaMontagne / August 4, 1945 / One page, 8vo.
2. The frontispiece—a photograph of Eisenhower taken about the time the letter was written.
3. The letter itself.
4. The original envelope bearing the censor's stamp and the signature of Lieutenant Colonel E. R. Lee, an Eisenhower aide.
5. The bill of sale from the dealer.
6. A letter from the dealer attesting to and guaranteeing the authenticity of Eisenhower's signature.

Your local five-and-ten is sure to offer a variety of ready-made photograph frames.

Other significant letters and documents can be similarly show-cased, with the accompanying material as varied and colorful as you wish to make it. Not only do albums of this type safely preserve items of consequence, they serve to add to their importance and increase your satisfaction of ownership.

Almost all collectors enjoy having special items framed for display. You can take a document to a framing shop and have it custom-framed (framing shops are listed in the Yellow Pages of your telephone directory under "Picture Frames—Dealers"), or you can buy a ready-made frame, called a photograph frame, at your local five-and-ten.

Ready-made frames are inexpensive. The 8″ x 10″ size, consisting of a black wooden frame, glass of matching size, cardboard backing, and a metal loop to use for hanging, costs about a dollar. The 11″ x 14″ size costs about $1.50.

Each frame also has a mat. A mat is a piece of cardboard, usually rectangular in shape, which goes between the item being framed and the glass. The mat is important, for not only does it serve as a border for the framed item, but by creating a space between the document and the glass, it protects the document from moisture that can form on the glass because of high humidity. Never frame a document so that it touches the glass; use a mat.

When using a ready-made frame, you simply remove the cardboard backing, insert the mat and the document, and then replace the backing. No pasting is necessary.

Many collectors decorate the mat. For instance, on the mat framing an autographed photo of Prime Minister Pierre Trudeau of Canada, you may wish to paste a color reproduction of the Canadian flag. (Use rubber cement for such gluing operations.) The mat used in framing General William Westmoreland's photograph might bear four gold stars, indicating his military rank, that of "four star" general. Some collectors affix biographical information to the mat.

When framing a person's signature, you may wish to include a photograph of the person within the frame. Neil Armstrong's signature might be framed along with a reproduction of a newspaper headline proclaiming his moon walk. Charles Schulz's autograph could be framed with a cutting from his comic strip, "Peanuts."

If you frame material behind glass, never hang it where it will be struck by the sun's rays. Sunlight, even a few hours of it, fades ink and discolors paper. Artificial light can be harmful, too, both from fluorescent tubes and the standard incandescent bulb. The former causes greater damage than the latter.

At the British Museum, reports *Manuscripts*, display cases are covered with strips of velvet material to protect the documents from artificial light. To view a document, the visitor must roll back the velvet.

If you want to frame and display a particularly valuable item, you should take certain precautionary measures. Instead of framing it behind ordinary glass, use specially tinted sheet plastic to screen out ultraviolet light. Plexiglass in the "F series" manufactured by the Rohm and Haas Company (Independence Mall West, Philadelphia, Pennsylvania 19105) is one recommended type. Write to the firm for more information, or inquire at your local framing shop about this specially tinted sheet plastic.

A few collectors have material laminated—pressed between a pair of thin plastic layers to form a single sheet—to preserve it. But lamination is not a usual method of preservation, and should only be considered in the case of a valuable document that is in such worn-out condition it no longer can be handled.

Laminating should only be done by an expert. Never consider using an office laminating machine or the type available at many photography shops. When a document is professionally laminated, the paper is first de-acidified and polished, and high quality laminating materials are used.

Use an Artgum eraser to re-move light smudges from autograph items.

No matter how you store valuable material, be on guard that the individual items are not kept in physical contact with "poor" paper, that is, paper that is high in acid content. Paper of this type can "infect" good paper, causing it to become brittle and discolor.

Perhaps at one time you have come upon a newspaper clipping that has been left between the pages of a book for a long time, for several years. Often the pages of the book touching the clipping will become stained brown in an area precisely the size of the clipping. This stain is caused by acid from the newsprint.

Virtually all paper made after 1900 contains these damaging acids, whether the paper is made of pulpwood or is all-rag paper. The acids are used in compounding the surface of the paper, not in the manufacture of the paper itself. And it is not only sheets of paper that contain these acids, but envelopes, file folders, cardboard, and other stationery products which collectors utilize.

If you have a particularly valuable document, use only acid-free paper (or the Mylar sheet protectors described above) in storing it. Ask at your local stationery store or paper distributing company about the availability of acid-free paper. Or you can write the Howard Division, St. Regis Paper Company (633 Third Avenue, New York, New York 10017) for more information.

Never attempt to repair a piece of autograph material yourself. Consult an expert. Amateurs who attempt to restore damaged material often cause additional damage.

If you have a valuable document that seems to require restoration, your local library may be helpful. A large library may have an experienced archivist on its staff who can give you advice. A few libraries do repair work on a free basis.

If the damage is minor, however, you can sometimes make the repairs yourself. You can, for example, remove folds, wrinkles, or curls from a sheet of paper with a simple flattening operation.

First, dampen the paper. At the National Archives in Washington, D. C., a room approximately ten feet square and equipped with powerful humidifiers is used to dampen documents. Your bathroom is somewhat comparable. Take the document to be flattened and place it on a stainless steel wire rack, the type used for cooling baked goods from the oven. Set the rack on the bathroom vanity or a high shelf—the higher the better. Run the hot water in the shower or tub until the room becomes steamy and the vapor causes the document to become limp.

As soon as the document has become thoroughly dampened, iron it. Use an electric iron. In adjusting the iron's flow of heat, consider the document to be a piece of "synthetic fabric." Use a piece of white blotting paper as your ironing base. The surface of the document must be protected from direct contact with the iron, so cover it with a sheet of white paper. Flatten out the document on the blotting paper. Be sure it is free of all wrinkles, even the smallest.

If the document being flattened is at all fragile, don't use an iron. After it is sufficiently dampened, place the document on a sheet of white blotting paper, cover it with a second sheet of blotting paper, and then weight down the "sandwich" with two or three heavy books. Keep the pressure on overnight.

Exposure to moisture for a short period in no way harms paper; in fact, in some cases it serves to strengthen it. Of course, too much moisture can be harmful. Never sponge or soak a document in your efforts to flatten out creases or wrinkles. Most modern inks dissolve in water, causing irreparable damage.

The repair you can do at home can also involve ordinary pencil marks or light smudges of dirt. Remove these with an Artgum eraser, available at any art supply store. When erasing, hold the paper firmly and make your strokes from the center of the sheet toward the edges.

Some collectors feel that even an Artgum eraser is too abrasive. Instead, they use small pieces of fresh, crustless bread to remove light smudges.

Be wary about using water or solvents to remove stains. Paste and certain types of glue can be sponged off with water, but bear in mind that coated paper can be damaged by coming in contact with water, and many types of ink are water-soluble. It is usually best to get the advice of an expert before you attempt to remove any type of stain.

Never tinker with an ink stain or try to restore faded ink. These, too, are problems for the experienced archivist.

During World War II, the cultural resources of many of the warring nations were subjected to serious damage. Experts at the National Archives in Washington, D. C., prepared a small handbook entitled *The Repair and Preservation of Records*, for distribution to libraries, museums, and other archival institutions whose collections were in risk of damage from enemy action.

The booklet, now considered one of the most authoritative handbooks on the subject of document repair and storage, is available at no charge from the National Archives and Records Service (Eighth Street and Pennsylvania Avenue, N.W., Washington, D. C. 20408) Write for a copy: ask for Bulletin No. 5.

Whenever you must mail autograph material—to a dealer for appraisal, for instance—carefully place each item between cardboard sheets and wrap the entire package. It is better to pack the wrapped material into a small carton than to use an envelope. With a carton you can be sure the material will not be folded or creased.

Never send a piece of framed material within its frame. The glass can break, in which case the document can be damaged or even cut by the glass fragments.

Always send autograph material by first class mail (except when you are mailing a book; then use the Special Fourth Class Rate for books).

Be sure to register the package or carton. Ask for a return receipt when you fill out the registration request form at the post office. The return receipt will cost you a few extra pennies in postage, but it's well worth it, for it serves to notify you that the mailed material has arrived at its destination.

If you are sending a considerable amount of material, inquire at your local Railway Express office about insured delivery service. Another delivery system—United Parcel Service—covers many parts of the country. Consult the Yellow Pages of your telephone directory to learn the names of still other services you might use. They are listed under "Delivery Services."

If your collection includes really valuable items, you should have it insured against loss due to fire or theft. It may, however, already be included under the terms of a homeowner's policy. One firm offers insurance protection to members of the Universal Autograph Collectors Club.

This advice will serve only as an introduction to the subject of caring for and displaying your autograph collection. There are many other sources of information.

If you visit New York City, make it a point to look in at the Charles Hamilton Galleries (25 East 53rd Street), the Antiquarian Booksellers Association of America (630 Fifth Avenue), or B. Altman & Company (Fifth Avenue at 34th Street), where you will see impressively framed autograph items on display. Collectors publications (*The Pen and Quill* and *Manuscripts*) feature articles on storing and exhibiting material on almost a regular basis. Dealers and other collectors are also a source of worthwhile information.

Appendix

AUTOGRAPH DEALERS

The firms listed below are the foremost of those in the United States and Canada that buy and sell autograph material. Those marked with an asterisk deal in material suitable for beginning collectors; they also issue free catalogs.

Abraham Lincoln Book Shop
18 East Chestnut Street
Chicago, Illinois 60611

Laurence C. Affron
711 South Flagler
West Palm Beach, Florida 33401

Bernard Amtmann, Inc.
750 Sherbrooke Street West
West Montreal, Canada

*Conway Barker
1231 Sunset Lane
Box 35
La Marque, Texas 77568

Robert Batchelder
1 West Butler Avenue
Ambler, Pennsylvania 19002

*David Battan, Autographs
Box 2212
Fresno, California 93720

Walter R. Benjamin, Autographs
790 Madison Avenue
New York, New York 10021

Robert K. Black
109 Lorraine Avenue
Upper Montclair, New Jersey 07043

Robert J. Boudwin
1119 Harker Avenue
Woodbury, New Jersey 08096

Wayne Bramble
2907 Fairlawn Street
Hillcrest Heights, Maryland 20031

Maury A. Bromsen Associates
195 Commonwealth Avenue
Boston, Massachusetts 02116

William J. B. Burger
12 East Holly Street
Pasadena, California 91101

Don Burnett
Box 178
East Greenwich,
Rhode Island 02818

*Carnegie Book Shop
140 East 59th Street
New York, New York 10022

Coins & Currency Inc.
29 South Eighteenth Street
Philadelphia, Pennsylvania 19103

*Herman M. Darvick
3109 Brighton 7th Street
Brooklyn, New York 11235

Emily Driscoll
175 Fifth Avenue
New York, New York 10010

Kendall G. Gaisser
1242 Broadway
Toledo, Ohio 43609

Bruce Gimelson, Autographs
Fort Washington Industrial Park
Fort Washington,
Pennsylvania 19034

Robert Golden
Box 61
Lathrup Village, Michigan 48015

*Goodspeed's Book Shop, Inc.
18 Beacon Street
Boston, Massachusetts 02108

Hamill & Barker
230 North Michigan Avenue
Chicago, Illinois 60601

*Charles Hamilton Autographs, Inc.
  25 East 53rd Street
  New York, New York 10022
*Doris Harris, Autographs
  6381 Hollywood Boulevard
  Los Angeles, California 90028
*Paul F. Hoag
  P.O. Box 257
  Weatogue, Connecticut 06089
King V. Hostick
  901 College Avenue
  Springfield, Illinois 62704
John Howell—Books
  434 Post Street
  San Francisco, California 94102
*Dr. Milton Kronovet
  75 Ocean Avenue
  Brooklyn, New York 11225
James Lowe
  219 East 70th Street
  New York, New York 10021
Howard Mott
  Sheffield, Massachusetts 01257
*Julie Sweet Newman
  Box 156
  Battle Creek, Michigan 49016

*Kenneth W. Rendell
  62 Bristol Road
  Somerville, Massachusetts 02144
*Paul C. Richards, Autographs
  233 Harvard Street
  Brookline, Massachusetts 02146
*George Rinsland
  4015 Kilmer Avenue
  Allerton, Pennsylvania 18104
*Joseph Rubenfine
  RFD #1
  Pleasantville, New Jersey 08232
The Scriptorium
  933 North LaCienega Boulevard
  Los Angeles, California 90069
Charles Sessler
  1308 Walnut Street
  Philadelphia, Pennsylvania 19107
Rosejeanne Slifer
  30 Park Avenue
  New York, New York 10016
William P. Wolfe
  222 rue de L'Hopital
  Montreal, Quebec
  Canada

CELEBRITY LIST

George Abbott (*producer, director, playwright*)
  630 Fifth Avenue
  New York, New York 10010

I. W. Abel (*labor union official*)
  United Steel Workers of America
  Commonwealth Building
  Pittsburgh, Pennsylvania 15241

Ralph Abernathy (*clergyman, civil rights leader*)
  Southern Christian Leadership Conference
  334 Auburn Avenue
  Atlanta, Georgia 30314

Major General Creighton W. Abrams (*U.S. Army officer*)
  U.S. Military Assistance Command
  APO San Francisco, California 96222

Conrad Aiken (*author*)
  "Forty-One Doors"
  Stony Brook Road
  Brewster, Massachusetts 02631

Woody Allen (*comedian, writer*)
  c/o Mike Hutner
  United Artists Corporation
  729 Seventh Avenue
  New York, New York 10019

Mario Andretti (*auto racer*)
c/o Sports Headliners, Inc.
4600 Georgetown Court
Speedway, Indiana 46222

Neil Armstrong (*astronaut*)
NASA Manned Spacecraft Center
Houston, Texas 77058

Eddy Arnold (*singer*)
c/o Gerard W. Purcell Associates
150 East 52nd Street
New York, New York 10022

Isaac Asimov (*writer*)
45 Greenough Street
West Newton, Massachusetts 02165

Lauren Bacall (*actress*)
c/o Peter Witt Associates
37 West 57th Street
New York, New York 10019

Joan Baez (*folk singer*)
Box 1001
Palo Alto, California 94302

Pearl Bailey (*singer, actress*)
c/o William Morris Agency
1350 Avenue of the Americas
New York, New York 10019

George Balanchine (*ballet dancer, choreographer*)
c/o School of American Ballet
144 West 66th Street
New York, New York 10023

Samuel Barber (*composer*)
609 Fifth Avenue
New York, New York 10022

Christiaan N. Barnard (*surgeon*)
Groote Schurr Hospital
Cape Town, South Africa

John Barth (*author*)
96 Beard Avenue
Buffalo, New York 14214

Saul Bellow (*author*)
University of Chicago
Chicago, Illinois 60637

Irving Berlin (*composer*)
1290 Sixth Avenue
New York, New York 10020

Leonard Bernstein (*composer, conductor*)
National Institute of Arts and Letters
205 West 57th Street
New York, New York 10022

Bill Blass (*fashion designer*)
550 Seventh Avenue
New York, New York 10018

Julian Bond (*civil rights leader*)
163 Euharlee Street
Atlanta, Georgia 30314

William F. Buckley (*editor, author, lecturer*)
National Review
150 East 35th Street
New York, New York 10016

Alexander Calder (*sculptor, artist*)
Sache, France

Truman Capote (*essayist, novelist*)
870 United Nations Plaza
New York, New York 10017

Pablo Casals (*violoncellist, composer, conductor*)
Festival Casals
Pda. 22,
Edif. Santurce
Santurce, Puerto Rico

Johnny Cash (*singer, musician, composer*)
Henderson, Tennessee 37075

Fidel Castro
Premier of Cuba
First Secretary of the Cuban Communist Party
Palacio del Gobierno
Havana, Cuba

Otis Chandler (*newspaper publisher*)
Los Angeles Times
Times Mirror Square
Los Angeles, California 90053

Van Cliburn (*concert pianist*)
c/o S. Hurok
730 Fifth Avenue
New York, New York 10019

Judy Collins (*folk singer*)
c/o Harold Leventhal
200 West 57th Street
New York, New York 10019

Aaron Copland (*composer*)
c/o Boosey & Hawkes Inc.
30 West 57th Street
New York, New York 10019

James Gould Cozzens (*author*)
Shadowbrook
Williamstown, Massachusetts 01267

142

Merce Cunningham (*choreographer, dancer*)
Merce Cunningham Studio
61 West 14th Street
New York, New York 10011

Salvador Dali (*Spanish surrealist painter*)
c/o M. Knoedler & Company
14 East 57th Street
New York, New York 10022

Michael E. De Bakey (*surgeon, professor*)
Baylor University College of Medicine
Houston, Texas 77025

Bob Dylan (*folk singer, composer, poet*)
c/o Albert B. Grossman Management
75 East 55th Street
New York, New York 10022

Charles Evers (*civil rights leader*)
Mississippi Field Office
National Association for the Advancement
    of Colored People
1072 Lynch Street
Jackson, Mississippi 39203

Jose Feliciano (*singer, guitarist*)
c/o Greif-Garris Management
8467 Beverly Boulevard
Los Angeles, California 90048

Bobby Fischer (*grand master of chess*)
560 Lincoln Place
Brooklyn, New York 11217

Peggy Fleming (*figure skating champion*)
c/o Bob Banner Associates
545 Madison Avenue
New York, New York 10022

Dame Margot Fonteyn (*ballerina*)
Royal Opera House
Covent Garden
London, W. 2. England

Aretha Franklin (*singer*)
1721 Field Street
Detroit, Michigan 48214

Theodor Seuss Geisel (*Dr. Seuss*)
7301 Encelia Drive
La Jolla, California 92037

Allen Ginsburg (*poet*)
c/o City Lights Books
261 Columbus Avenue
San Francisco, California 94133

John Glenn (*astronaut*)
Royal Crown Cola Company
545 Madison Avenue
New York, New York 10022

Martha Graham (*choreographer, director, teacher*)
3060 Buena Vista Way
Berkeley, California 94708

Roy Ellsworth Harris (*composer*)
1200 Tellem Drive
Pacific Palisades, California 90272

Jascha Heifetz (*violinist*)
1520 Gilcrest Drive
Beverly Hills, California 90210

Katherine Hepburn (*actress*)
201 Bloomfield Avenue
West Hartford, Connecticut 06117

Dustin Hoffman (*actor*)
67 West 55th Street
New York, New York 10019

Vladimir Horowitz (*pianist*)
c/o Columbia Records
799 Seventh Avenue
New York, New York 10019

Robert Joffrey (*choreographer, director, dancer*)
American Ballet Center
434 Avenue of the Americas
New York, New York 10011

Jasper Johns (*artist*)
340 Riverside Drive
New York, New York 10025

Philip Johnson (*architect*)
Ponus Street
New Canaan, Connecticut 06840

Tom Jones (*singer*)
c/o AMA Ltd.
24/25 New Bond Street
London, W. 1., England

Coretta King (*civil rights leader*)
234 Sunset Avenue N.W.
Atlanta, Georgia 30314

John V. Lindsay
Mayor of the City of New York
Gracie Mansion
New York, New York

Helen MacInnes (*writer*)
535 Park Avenue
New York, New York 10021

Norman Mailer (*essayist, novelist*)
c/o Scott Meredith Inc.
580 Fifth Avenue
New York, New York 10036

Bernard Malamud (*author*)
   c/o Russell & Volkening
   551 Fifth Avenue
   New York, New York 10017

Alicia Markova (*ballerina*)
   Metropolitan Opera House
   Lincoln Center Plaza
   New York, New York 10023

Mary McCarthy (*author*)
   c/o Brandt & Brandt
   101 Park Avenue
   New York, New York 10017

Steve McQueen (*actor*)
   c/o Paramount Pictures Theatres Corp.
   150 Broadway
   New York, New York 10036

Yehudi Menuhin (*violinist*)
   c/o Columbia Artists Management Inc.
   Cami Building
   165 W. 57th Street
   New York, New York 10019

David Merrick (*theatrical producer*)
   246 West 44th Street
   New York, New York 10036

Robert Merrill (*opera and concert singer*)
   Metropolitan Opera Associates
   Lincoln Center
   New York, New York 10023

Arthur Miller (*author, playwright*)
   c/o MCA Ltd.
   598 Madison Avenue
   New York, New York 10022

Henry Miller (*author*)
   Big Sur, California 93920

Joan Miro (*artist, sculptor*)
   13 rue de Teheran
   Galerie Maeght
   Paris 8e France

Robert Motherwell (*artist, lecturer*)
   c/o Sidney Janis Gallery
   15 East 57th Street
   New York, New York 10022

Daniel Patrick Moynihan (*sociologist, educator, author*)
   Joint Center for Urban Studies of the Massachusetts
      Institute of Technology and Harvard University
   66 Church Street
   Cambridge, Massachusetts 02138

Ralph Nader (*lawyer, author*)
53 Hillside Avenue
Winsted, Connecticut 06098

Rudolf Nureyev (*ballet dancer*)
Villa La Turbie
Monte Carlo, Monaco

Jacqueline Kennedy Onassis
1040 Fifth Avenue
New York, New York 10028

Eugene Ormandy (*conductor, violinist*)
230 South 15th Street
Philadelphia, Pennsylvania 19102

Pope Paul VI
Supreme Pontiff of the Roman Catholic Church
Vatican City

Jan Peerce (*opera and concert singer*)
c/o Maurice Feldman
745 Fifth Avenue
New York, New York 10022

I. M. Pei (*architect*)
I. M. Pei & Partners
600 Madison Avenue
New York, New York 10022

Katherine Anne Porter (*author*)
3601 49th Street N.W.
Washington, D. C. 20016

Leontyne Price (*concert and opera singer*)
1133 Broadway
New York, New York 10010

Anthony Quinn (*actor*)
333 Las Casas Avenue
Pacific Palisades, California 90272

His Serene Highness Prince Rainier III
Palais de Monaco
Monte Carlo, Monaco

Jerome Robbins (*choreographer, director*)
17 51st Street
Weehawken, New Jersey 07087

Richard Rodgers (*composer*)
c/o Rodgers & Hammerstein
598 Madison Avenue
New York, New York 10022

Artur Rubinstein (*pianist*)
630 Park Avenue
New York, New York 10021

146

Howard Rusk (*physician, medical writer*)
Institute of Rehabilitation Medicine
New York University Medical Center
400 East 34th Street
New York, New York 10016

Bayard Rustin (*civil rights leader, lecturer*)
A. Philip Randolph Institute
217 West 125th Street
New York, New York 10027

Jim Ryun (*champion runner*)
Athletic Department
University of Kansas
Lawrence, Kansas 66044

Albert B. Sabin (*physician*)
400 Rawson Woods Lane
Cincinnati, Ohio 45220

J. D. Salinger (*author*)
c/o Harold Ober
40 E 49th Street
New York, New York 10017

Jonas E. Salk (*bacteriologist*)
Salk Institute for Biological Studies
Box 1809
San Diego, California 92112

William Howard Schumann (*composer*)
Lincoln Center for The Performing Arts
1865 Broadway
New York, New York 10023

Martin Schwarzschild (*astronomer, astrophysicist*)
Princeton Observatory
Princeton University
Princeton, New Jersey 08540

Maurice Sendak (*writer, illustrator*)
29 West 9th Street
New York, New York 10011

Rudolf Serkin (*pianist*)
R.F.D. 3
Brattleboro, Vermont 05301

Anne Sokolow (*choreographer, director, teacher*)
1 Christopher Street
New York, New York 10014

Susan Sontag (*writer*)
c/o Farrar, Straus & Giroux
19 Union Square West
New York, New York 10003

Eleanor Steber (*concert and opera singer*)
105 W 55th Street
New York, New York 10019

Isaac Stern (*violinist*)
730 Fifth Avenue
New York, New York 10022

Leopold Stokowski (*orchestra conductor*)
1067 5th Avenue
New York, New York 10028

Irving Stone (*author*)
1360 Summitridge Place
Beverly Hills, California 90210

Barbra Streisand (*singer*)
48 East 80th Street
New York, New York 10020

William Styron (*author*)
R.F.D.
Roxbury, Connecticut 06783

Arthur Ochs Sulzberger (*newspaper publisher*)
The New York Times
229 West 43rd Street
New York, New York 10036

Joan Sutherland (*concert and opera singer*)
c/o Colbert Artists Management
850 7th Avenue
New York, New York 10019

Maria Tallchief (*ballerina*)
c/o New York City Ballet Company
Lincoln Center for the Performing Arts
New York, New York 10023

Edward Teller (*physicist*)
University of California Radiation Laboratory
Box 808
Livermore, California 94550

Harry S Truman (*former president*)
Independence, Missouri

Richard Tucker (*concert and opera singer*)
Columbia Artists Management, Inc.
165 W 57th Street
New York, New York, 10019

John Updike (*writer*)
26 East Street
Ipswich, Massachusetts 10938

Violette Verdy (*ballerina*)
c/o New York City Ballet Company
Lincoln Center for the Performing Arts
New York, New York 10023

Kurt Vonnegut, Jr. (*author*)
Scudder's Lane
West Barnstable, Massachusetts 02668

Andy Warhol (*artist*)
1342 Lexington Avenue
New York, New York 10029

Robert Penn Warren (*author*)
2495 Redding Road
Fairfield, Connecticut 06430

Dionne Warwick (*singer*)
c/o Sceptre Records Inc.
254 West 54th Street
New York, New York 10019

Charles Weidman (*choreographer, director, dancer*)
144 W 55th Street
New York, New York 10019

General William Westmoreland
Chief of Staff U.S. Army
The Pentagon
Washington, D. C.

Roy Wilkins (*civil rights leader*)
National Association for the Advancement of Colored People
1790 Broadway
New York, New York 10019

Tennessee Williams (*American playwright*)
c/o Audrey Wood
555 Madison Avenue
New York, New York 10022

Andrew Wyeth (*artist*)
Chadds Ford, Pennsylvania 19317

Minoru Yamasaki (*architect*)
3077 Livernois Road
Troy, Michigan 48084

For Additional Reading

Benjamin, Mary. *Autographs: A Key to Collecting.* New York: R. R. Bowker Company, 1946.

Hamilton, Charles. *Collecting Autographs and Manuscripts.* Norman, Oklahoma: University of Oklahoma Press, 1961.

———. *Scribblers and Scoundrels.* New York: Paul S. Eriksson, 1968.

———. *The Robot That Helped to Make a President.* New York: Charles Hamilton, 1965.

Madigan, Thomas. *Word Shadows of the Great.* New York: Frederick A. Stokes, 1930.

Notlep, Robert. *Autograph Collecting: A New Guide.* New York: Crown Publishers, 1968.

Taylor, John M. *From the White House Inkwell: American Presidential Autographs.* Rutland, Vermont: Charles Tuttle & Company.

Index